T0324494

CAMBRIDGE SERIES ON HUMAN–COMPUTER INTERACTION

The Computer User as Toolsmith

The Use, Reuse, and Organization
of Computer-based Tools

Cambridge Series on Human–Computer Interaction

Managing Editor:
Professor J. Long, Ergonomics Unit, University College, London

Editorial Board
Dr. P. Barnard, Medical Research Council, Applied Psychology Unit, Cambridge, England.
Professor W. Buxton, Rank Xerox Ltd, Cambridge EuroPARC, England.
Dr. J. M. Carroll, IBM Thomas J. Watson Research Center, Yorktown Heights, New York.
Dr. J. Grudin, MCC, Austin, Texas.
Dr. T. Landauer, Bellcore, Morristown, New Jersey.
Professor J. Lansdown, CASCAAD, Middlesex Polytechnic, England.
Professor T. W. Malone, MIT, Cambridge, Massachusetts.
Professor H. Thimbleby, Department of Computing Science, University of Stirling, England.
Professor T. Winograd, Department of Computer Science, Stanford University, California.

The Computer User as Toolsmith

The Use, Reuse, and Organization of Computer-based Tools

Saul Greenberg
University of Calgary

CAMBRIDGE
UNIVERSITY PRESS

CAMBRIDGE UNIVERSITY PRESS
Cambridge, New York, Melbourne, Madrid, Cape Town,
Singapore, São Paulo, Delhi, Mexico City

Cambridge University Press
The Edinburgh Building, Cambridge CB2 8RU, UK

Published in the United States of America by Cambridge University Press, New York

www.cambridge.org
Information on this title: www.cambridge.org/9780521404303

© Cambridge University Press 1993

This publication is in copyright. Subject to statutory exception
and to the provisions of relevant collective licensing agreements,
no reproduction of any part may take place without the written
permission of Cambridge University Press.

First published 1993

A catalogue record for this publication is available from the British Library

Library of Congress Cataloguing in Publication Data
Greenberg, Saul.
The Computer user as toolsmith. The use, reuse, and organization of
computer-based tools
     p.   cm. – (Cambridge series on human–computer interaction ;
[6])
Includes bibliographical references.
ISBN 0521-40430-4
1. Human-computer interaction.   2. UNIX (Computer file)
I. Title   II. Series.
QA76.9H85G73   1993
004´,01´9–dc20   92-24677
                                                              CIP

ISBN 978-0-521-40430-3 Hardback

Cambridge University Press has no responsibility for the persistence or
accuracy of URLs for external or third-party internet websites referred to in
this publication, and does not guarantee that any content on such websites is,
or will remain, accurate or appropriate. Information regarding prices, travel
timetables, and other factual information given in this work is correct at
the time of first printing but Cambridge University Press does not guarantee
the accuracy of such information thereafter.

Contents

List of figures

List of tables

Foreword

Humans are the most versatile of creatures, and computers are their most versatile of creations. Human–Computer Interaction (HCI) is the study of what they do together; in particular, HCI aims to make interaction better suit the humans. Computers contribute to art, science, engineering, . . . all areas of human endeavor. It is no surprise, then, that there is heated debate about what the essence of HCI is and what it should be. What is good HCI? The answer to this question will be elusive given that there is good engineering that is not art, good art that is not science, and good science that is not engineering.

It's easier to see what form of answer there can be by taking a quick excursion into another field. Imagine the discovery of a dye, such as W. H. Perkin's breakthrough discovery of mauve. Is it science? Yes: certain chemicals must react to produce the dyestuff, and the principles of chemistry suggest other possibilities. Is it art? Yes: it makes an attractive color. Is it engineering? Yes: its quantity production, fastness in materials, and so forth, are engineering. Perkin's work made the once royal purple accessible to all. Fortunately there is no subject "Human Chemical Interaction" to slide us into thinking that there is, or should be, one right view of the work of making or using, designing, standardizing, or evaluating a dye. Nevertheless, we appreciate a readily available, stunning color, used by an able artist, and one that lasts without deteriorating. What is good, then, put briefly, is what is made accessible, reliable, worthwhile.

By analogy: a good contribution to the field of Human–Computer Interaction is *accessible* (its principles should work for others and repeatably, potentially by being computerized), *reliable* (it should work under prescribed conditions), and *worthwhile* (it should do something beneficial, applicable, appealing). One also requires that these qualities are *demonstrable*, not only to distinguish fact from fancy, but so that practitioners can assess whether the contribution is relevant and applicable to their particular concerns.

Saul Greenberg's *The Computer User as Toolsmith* starts from the observation that humans tend to repeat themselves, and that this is a general phenomenon that can be studied, understood, and facilitated. It follows that tools used for repeated activities are themselves reused, and thus that it is desirable to improve the tools of reuse. The results reported in this book are accessible: but more so, the book indicates how anyone could access the equivalent results in their own particular circumstances. This is a broader and more valuable accessibility. In short, reuse is accessible to anyone who cares to look. It is further a reliable phenomenon, and is shown to be so by the studies reported here. Finally, to the extent that a computer can support and simplify reuse, the concepts are very widely applicable. Greenberg shows that supporting reuse can be staightforwardly built into interactive computer systems, and to do so is worthwhile. This is the book's contribution to engineering beyond the particular experiments and systems described here.

We gave criteria for good HCI above; this book meets them. It identifies reuse as a single, core concept (like aniline dye) and demonstrates its generality for HCI. When computer systems are engineered that embed appropriate facilities for supporting reuse then, as Greenberg demonstrates, they are quantifiably improved.

As well as making a useful and focused contribution to HCI, this book is its author's doctoral dissertation. As such it also makes a good example of what a dissertation can be, particularly in the interdisciplinary and currently uncertain area of HCI. There is an idea, refined to a hypothesis, and it is checked in various guises. Systems are built. And ideas are rechecked, both by appeal to the literature and by data from the use of other systems that had nothing to do with the author's work. The work is described clearly: the book is aware of what it is achieving and its relation to wider issues in HCI – this greatly adds to the pleasure of reading it. There is sufficient detail for the interested reader to repeat experiments and check methods, or, more likely, to progress confidently from where Greenberg leaves off.

Many other dissertations (books too) describe ideas or systems that, however much they inspire, still leave the next researcher almost as much work to repeat – and occasionally a nagging suspicion that some of the work is unrepeatable, even imaginary where it is most inspiring! In the breadth of HCI there is ample scope for inspirational creativity, but far better to share the means to the ends. The ideas of this book are creative *and* they work, and there is both ample evidence and argument why. That is good for a dissertation. Even better for HCI, the topic is of such universal applicability that the book is the starting point for evaluating and improving almost any existing or future system. The book itself is a tool that can and should be reused.

Harold Thimbleby
Stirling, Scotland

Acknowledgments and dedication

The research described in this book is the result of my dissertation work. My supervisor Ian Witten struck the fine balance of guiding my research without hindering my own expression and development of ideas. He encouraged me to learn, to explore, and to publish. As the legendary "Witten filter," he transformed even my worst writings into acceptable prose. He set high standards, but never hesitated to show the steps necessary to reach them.

David Hill introduced me to human–computer interaction, encouraged my research endeavours, and was always available as a tried and true resource. I was kept constantly on my toes by Brian Gaines and Harold Thimbleby, who made the field a moving target with their constant twists and paradigm shifts. It was Harold who encouraged me to transform the dissertation into a book.

Of course there is my family. The faith, love, and support of my wife Judy kept me going through all the slow academic and writing times. My research lifestyle was balanced by our many outdoor adventures, where her cheerfulness and enthusiasm always shone through. Our son Adam, whose birth and growth paralled this book, was another avid supporter. No matter how tiring the day was, his ready laughter when I returned home always filled me with joy.

But this book is dedicated to my parents, Morris and Bella Greenberg. Because of their religion and the oppressive Eastern European politics of their childhoods, they had no opportunity for advanced education. Yet they never failed to see its importance, and always encouraged me to pursue its path.

1

Introduction

There is nothing quite so frustrating for the avid do-it-yourselfer than to begin a project, suddenly need a particular tool, but have no idea where in the house to look for it.
— *Practical Homeowner's 1987 Do-It-Yourself Annual*

General-purpose computer environments that furnish a large set of diverse tools are often hard to use. Although some difficulty is associated with using any particular tool, this book is concerned with the problems that a person faces when *selecting* a tool from the many available, *reusing* that tool while performing a task, and *organizing* the chosen tools in a way that makes them ready to hand later on. Surprisingly, methods and habits for using physical tools that have evolved over millions of years have not been transferred effectively to the computer domain.

The goal of the research discussed in this book is to identify properties of a human–computer interface that supports how people select, reuse, and organize the tools available in general-purpose computing environments. These properties come from empirical analyses of user behavior. This introduction sets the scene first by reviewing physical tools, from their very natural use by animals to ultra sophisticated machinery that taxes human capabilities beyond acceptable performance limits. Section 1.2 moves to the focus of this book – general-purpose computing environments that make diverse collections of on-line tools available. It identifies two problem areas: the dearth of knowledge about people's use of on-line tools, and the poor existing user support for everyday interactions with them. The final section outlines the major themes covered by each of the following chapters.

1.1 Using physical tools

Until the late eighteenth century, humans distinguished themselves from other animals by claiming to be the only tool-users. Since then, ethologists have reported extensive tool use by many species of animals. A few examples follow.[1]

The *myrmicine ant* drops debris (bits of leaf and bark) on to soft foods that are otherwise difficult to move. After all the food has soaked into the "sponge tool," it is carried back to the colony (Fellers and Fellers, 1976). The Egyptian vulture

---

[1] The definitive treatment of tool use by animals is Benjamin Beck's *Animal Tool Behaviour* (Beck, 1980). Unless stated otherwise, all references to tool use by animals and early humans reported in this section are taken from Beck's extensive catalog.

Figure 1.1. The Galapagos finch probing for insects with a cactus spine.
Illustration by J. Poehlman, in Smullen, 1978, p. 17.

feeds on tough-shelled ostrich eggs by picking up a stone in its bill and throwing it down repeatedly until the egg cracks (van Lawick-Goodall and van Lawick, 1968). Figure 1.1 illustrates the well-known woodpecker finch of the Galapagos Islands. Using twigs and cactus spines held in its bill, the finch probes for otherwise unattainable insects living in trees or under bark.

The elephant is a frequent tool-user too. Twigs and branches grasped in its trunk extend its reach, particularly for scratching and chasing away flies, and the elephant also threatens intruders by waving branches or by throwing "missiles" at them. Sea otters break open shells by pounding them on rocks that are balanced on their chests (Hall and Schaller, 1964). Excluding humans, primates are the most habitual tool-users of all animals. Depending on the species, untrained monkeys, apes, and chimpanzees throw or drop things (stones, branches) at intruders, use leaves as sponges to gather water, brandish sticks as clubs, wipe wounds with leaves, and use various implements to pound open, extend their reach toward, or probe and rake in food. The extensive tool behavior of captive chimpanzees is evident to any circus or zoo visitor. They stack and climb upon objects to reach food, and they have been trained to ride bicycles.

Humans cannot even claim to be the only species that manufactures tools. Although most animals obtain tools from the natural debris of their environment, a few also fabricate them. Beck (1980) recognized four modes of tool manufacture in animals. The first is *detach*, as performed by a woodpecker finch breaking off its twig tool from branches. An example of *subtract*, the second mode, is when a parrot removes bark from a twig before scratching himself, or when chimpanzees strip leaves from branches before digging for termites. Some chimpanzees are known to *reshape* pieces of wood into tools with pointed tips by chewing. Finally, implements can be *combined*, although this has been observed only with captive animals. Chimpanzees, for example, join sticks together to create a further-reaching tool.

Although humans cannot lay claim to exclusive tool use and manufacture, humans do distinguish themselves by the complexity of their tools, how they are used and reused, and how they interrelate. First, humans are the only animals known who use one tool to produce another. This behavior is believed to date back 2,500,000 years to our hominid ancestors who whittled wooden tools with sharp flakes of stone (Leakey and Lewin, 1978). Second, humans retain tools for repeated reuse, unlike most animals who discard them immediately after use.[2] Again, early hominid records indicate that stone tools were transported from foreign fabrication locations and then used extensively before being discarded. Third, humans use tools at special-purpose sites. Early hominids had special food preparation areas, and archeological evidence from later periods shows much tool-based activity around the hearth and well-lit work areas (Gowlett, 1984). The final distinguishing point of human tool use arises when tools become more numerous and more diverse over the course of history. One only has to step into a modern kitchen or handyman's workshop for proof.

The present age heralds unprecedented availability of numerous tools for individual use. Some, like the hammer, are simple refinements of our ancestor's stone implements. At the other extreme are machines – examples are airplanes and spacecraft – that are so complex that only a few highly trained individuals can use them. During World War II, human ability was pushed beyond acceptable performance limits by the difficulty of using these complex machines. Some aircraft accidents, for example, were directly attributed to cockpit complexity. This resulted in a demand for experts in psychological engineering – called *human factors* in North America, and *ergonomics* in Europe – who recognize human limitations and apply their knowledge to the design of effective human–machine systems (Fitts, 1951). One area of human factors involves designing and simplifying tools that are inherently complex. For example, the highly interrelated controls and gauges in large power plants are often positioned on a map that mimics the physical location of their corresponding devices, making the plant's state easier to understand. Another area of concern – and the theme of this book – is the difficulty of using and managing large collections of loosely related tools.

When a person's activity is highly dynamic or not readily specified, the actual

---

[2]One of the few reported cases of tool retention by animals is the otter, which sometimes keeps shell-cracking stones in its armpit between several successive feeds while diving for other shells (Hall and Schaller, 1964).

choice and arrangements of loosely related tools cannot be effectively predicted by another person. Instead, people have general methods for structuring their workspaces, and special "organizing tools" for gathering and locating tools and materials. The following list indicates a few important strategies.

Recently used tools are available for reuse.   People recognize when a tool just used will be used again in the near future. Rather than select tools and then immediately return them to their original location, they are kept on hand for a period of time. Examples include retaining used cooking implements on counters while preparing a meal, and keeping a dictionary and thesaurus on a desk while writing.

Arranging tools by function.   Tools are categorized by function, and each collection is gathered separately. A mechanic, for example, uses the drawers in a tool cabinet to organize wrenches, screwdrivers, ratchets, and sockets. The office worker may arrange a desk with a pen and pencil holder, a stationary drawer, and a forms drawer. A tailor uses pin cushions, racks for holding spools of thread, shelves for bolts of cloth, and boxes for sewing machine accessories.

Arranging tools by task.   People sometimes store together tools that address a particular repetitive task. Workbenches and the tools located on them in a large carpenter's shop may reflect specialized activities; cutting (power saw, blades, fences), preparation (large table, glue, vice, clamps, finishing nails), drilling (drill, bits), nailing (work belt with hammer and nail pouches), and so on.

The idealized carpenter's workshop in Figure 1.2 illustrates an integrated use of these management strategies. Recently used tools and material lying on the central workbench are readily available for reuse. The tool cabinet and tool panels arrange tools by function, whereas other work areas are dedicated to certain tasks.

1.2   Soft tools in general-purpose computing environments

1.2.1   Definitions

Some important terms are introduced here. Others are defined and elaborated as needed throughout the book.

A *shell* is the top-level interface placed upon a general-purpose computing environment (the characteristics of these environments are discussed further in Section 1.2.2). A shell allows users to access a library of existing programs as utilities, to combine existing utilities as needed, and to extend the library at will. An *activity* or *submission* is defined as a single request submitted to the shell by a person. Activities typically specify actions and arguments. *Actions* are commands that indicate

Figure 1.2. An idealized carpenter's workshop, adapted from p. 51 in
Working in Wood, by E. Scott, Putnam, NY, 1980.

the utility to be invoked. *Arguments* supply information to the utility, through *options* that dictate how it is to work, and *objects* that indicate the computer material to be manipulated. *Incremental interaction* is a style of human–computer dialog characterized by successive activity requests that are submitted to the shell and responded to in turn (Thimbleby, 1990, p. 55). A computer *tool* is another name for a system utility. However, a user may consider the tool to include specific arguments as well.

Interfaces to conventional operating systems provide good examples of incremental interaction dialogs involving all the notions above. One usually submits activities to a top-level command shell by typing simple commands and arguments, although some modern systems augment or replace this primitive dialog style with menus, forms, natural language, graphics, and so on (Witten and Greenberg, 1985). The user then waits for the utility to do its task before entering the next submission.

1.2.2   *From appliances to manufacturing*

Computers and their uses fall under an enormous variety of often overlapping categories. They range from dedicated turnkey "appliances," specialized tools that address highly specific domains, to interactive programming and computing environments that function as software "manufacturing" plants. This book is concerned only with those general, flexible, and heterogeneous computer environments whose shells provide end-users with many diverse tools and materials, selected through incremental interaction. These environments lie somewhere between the extremes above.

The design emphasis in human–computer interfaces for the non-programming mass market is currently on application areas perceived to be used frequently by the target population. There is a proliferation of packages for word processing, painting and drafting, spreadsheet calculations, and so on. These packages may be considered appliances, highly specialized tools handling very specific tasks. Some have excellent interfaces that are finely tuned to meet specific user needs. Modern appliance-oriented top-level interfaces, augmented with a limited repertory of generic capabilities, act as delivery vehicles for these application packages (e.g., the Apple Macintosh; Williams, 1984). However, those users who do not wish to program may pursue only the relatively small set of tasks addressed by the applications that are provided. This poses appreciable difficulties.

> Computers are increasingly used ... in complex areas ... characterized by the lack of generally accepted methods and techniques to be used for problem solving. For this reason it is impossible to construct software tools covering problem solving completely.
>
> — Dzida, Hoffmann, and Valder, 1987, p. 30

At the other end of the spectrum, programming environments provide users with the means to pursue goals not addressed specifically by any one application. Historically, these systems arose from the second- and third-generation computers that emphasized programming in high-level languages (Denning, 1971). Their contemporary versions are highly interactive programming environments that simplify programming "in the small." Some examples are: SMALLTALK (Goldberg, 1984); INTERLISP–D (Teitelman and Masinter, 1981); PICT (Glinert and Tanimoto, 1984); and PECAN (Reiss, 1984). By analogy, these programming environments are highly sophisticated manufacturing plants that can be retooled rapidly to design and create a variety of complex machinery.

Although appliance environments are overly restrictive for those wishing to pursue general tasks, programming environments are impractical for nonprogrammers, for the actions, objects, and complexity of discourse are expressed in unfamiliar programming terms (Cuff, 1980). The computer industry is not blind to this incompatibility, and has spent considerable effort trying to bridge the gap between specialization and generalization through *integrated* systems. This approach groups a set of limited applications into one large integrated product, so that the boundaries between these applications are minimized or eliminated (Nielsen, Mack, Bergendorff, and Grischkowsky, 1986). These systems, although a promising direction, currently offer only slightly more power than appliance-oriented computers.

Midway between the two extremes are those top-level interfaces that provide their end-users with a rich set of actions and objects. Each action, together with the object it manipulates, is available as a tool, and the tools can be combined in simple ways to manufacture new tools, often without resorting to conventional programming. The use and organization of these types of tools form the focus of this book. As summarized by Lee, environments in this general-purpose computer genre include

> collections of heterogeneous but complementary tools that allow users to perform a wide and varying range of tasks. Furthermore, the environment provides fairly uniform access to the software tools and permits users to use them for various purposes.
> — Lee, 1988

Generally, tools are flexible to use, can be combined in many ways, and are reshaped as needed. In addition, these environments support and encourage both tool manufacture and sharing by a variety of end-users.

1.2.3 Problem statement

The hypothesis of the research reported in this book is that, as with physical tools, people select and often immediately reuse their recently submitted activities to general-purpose computing environments, and consciously organize their activities by both task and function. If this hypothesis holds, then the interface should give the user support by keeping recently used activities available for reuse and by allowing the user to organize activities by function or task.

Yet existing shells invariably provide either uniform access to all system utilities or group them in a predefined way. Except for a few ad hoc and unevaluated implementations, there is no on-line support by even contemporary interfaces for people's natural strategies for organizing their workspace. Command-based interfaces, for example, provide uniform access to all system actions, even though actual usage of these commands is far from uniform. "History systems" that allow people to recall old submissions are badly designed, and their effectiveness is unknown. Menus that explicitly reveal pregrouped system actions may not reflect the user's actual task organization.

This research addresses two major problems. First, there is a dearth of knowledge of how users actually behave when interacting with a general-purpose environment. Second, current interfaces do not adequately support a user's natural work. Although some have studied how people choose system utilities from a large set, no statistics are available on how people generate, select, and repeat their activities. The bulk of this work is devoted to filling this void, based upon analyses of long-term observations made of people using UNIX,[3] a general-purpose computing environment. The experimental findings are then generalized and used to derive design principles of a user support facility that aids natural work.

1.3 Outline

The book is divided into four distinct parts. Chapters 2 and 3 list how observations of user activity in general-purpose computing environments have been collected and analyzed in the past. The particular method employed in our research is described, and selected previous works are replicated and the findings are discussed. Chapters 4 through 7 form the heart of the book. They detail how people repeat their activities, and how the results can be applied to designing a facility that lets one reuse (as opposed to reenter) previous submissions. Chapter 8 examines how people organize activities. Finally, Chapter 9 describes the design and implementation of a user support tool that allows people to both reuse and impose a structure upon their old activities. Each chapter is briefly summarized below.

Chapter 2 introduces a study of natural everyday human usage of the UNIX operating system and its command line interface. The observations made are the basis for most investigative work performed in later chapters. UNIX is argued to be a general-purpose environment and therefore appropriate for observation.

---

[3]UNIX is a trademark of AT&T Bell Laboratories.

After several existing data collection methodologies are described, the one finally employed is detailed.

Chapter 3 covers previous work on how people use commands in UNIX. The results of several studies are reviewed, and portions of these studies are replicated. Although the statistical details of the replicated studies are supported, some of the conclusions made by the original researchers are misleading. In particular, studying command use – the verbs of a command line – is not sufficient and presents a distorted view of what actually occurs. The complete command line entered by the user must be considered too.

Chapter 4 introduces and surveys existing reuse facilities that let users recall, modify, and resubmit their previous entries to computers. Although the survey is not exhaustive, it is representative of facilities on commercial, state of the art, and research systems. The chapter concludes by noting that there is no empirical evidence justifying any of these designs, either a priori through knowledge of how people repeat activities, or post hoc by evaluating their actual use.

Chapter 5 continues by providing empirical evidence that people not only repeat their activities, but that they do so in quite regular ways. It starts with the notion of *recurrent systems*, where most users predominantly repeat their previous activities. A few suspected recurrent systems from both non-computer and computer domains are examined in this context to help pinpoint salient features. The UNIX data is analyzed from this perspective, with particular attention being paid to the statistics of complete command line recurrences. Although people are seen to generate many new activities, old ones are repeated to a surprising degree. The probability distribution of the next submission repeating a previous one as a function of recency is also reported.

Chapter 6 considers the potential and actual reuse opportunities within UNIX. First, several methods are suggested that could increase the likelihood that the next submission occurs in a small set of predictions offered to the user for review and reuse. The UNIX data is conditioned by these methods, and the resulting improvements are determined quantitatively. The second part of the chapter investigates how well the reuse facilities supplied by the UNIX shell are used in practice.

Chapter 7 summarizes the results as a set of design principles, and existing reuse facilities are revisited and briefly criticized from this perspective. The findings of previous chapters are then corroborated by analyzing a different domain – a functional programming environment – as a recurrent system. A final discussion concludes that the notion of reuse facilities is conceptually, as well as empirically, justified as a user support tool.

Chapter 8 argues that a user organizes computer activities by task and by function. The concept of a user support tool called a *workspace* is developed. Similar to a physical workspace, this on-line facility allows people to reuse and organize their tools for their related activities. Although the idea is not new, several novel properties of workspaces are elaborated. This chapter reveals how limited our knowledge is in this area and suggests that much more investigative research is required – work that is beyond the scope of this book.

Chapter 9 describes the design of a system that loosely follows the metaphor of a handyman's workbench. It embodies the reuse properties suggested in Chapters 4 through 7, and the structuring properties of Chapter 8. The implementation is a front end to UNIX, and serves to illustrate that serious pragmatic problems are encountered when user support tools are built as add-ons to existing systems. The problems encountered during the system's design and use indicate a few open research areas.

The book ends with a brief chapter. The contributions are summarized, implications to modern direct manipulation interfaces are discussed, and future research directions are proposed.

2

Studying UNIX

This chapter introduces a study of natural everyday human usage of the UNIX operating system and its command line interface. Analysis of the data collected is central to the pursuit of knowledge of user behavior when interacting with general-purpose environments. The chapter begins by describing UNIX and gives reasons why it is an appropriate vehicle for research. Section 2.2 reviews several methods of data collection used with previous UNIX investigations, and Section 2.3 describes the details of the current study. Analyses of data are deferred to later chapters.

2.1 Choosing UNIX

Why perform natural studies on UNIX, with its baroque and outdated user interface, instead of controlled experiments on a modern system? This section starts by advocating a natural study for exploratory investigation of human–computer interaction. After recognizing several pragmatic problems with such investigations, UNIX is introduced and its choice is justified.

2.1.1 Natural studies

The thrust of the work presented in this book is that it is possible to capitalize on patterns evident in human–computer interaction by building special user support tools. A prerequisite is to "know the user" (Hansen, 1971). One way to accomplish this goal is through analyzing everyday natural user interactions with current systems so that existing patterns of activity can be discovered and exploited. Hanson, Kraut, and Farber (1984) justify this approach by contrast with traditional controlled experimentation.

> Although [a controlled experiment is] appropriate and useful in theory-guided research ... it is less appropriate when the researcher needs to identify new variables or complex unknown relations between new variables. Nor does it deal efficiently with highly multivariate phenomena such as human–computer interaction. Where neither theory nor time will tolerate the isolation of a few controlling variables, assessing people's natural use of a computer system may be highly informative. ... Generally, observational data of human–computer interaction can allow the testing of simple hypotheses and intuitions, the discovery of computer features that cause problems for users, and guidelines for interface design.
> — Hanson, Kraut, and Farber, 1984

Investigating people's natural behavior when using computer systems is not

11

easy. Several major problems present themselves. First, there is no established methodology of study. Past experimenters used various methods, leading not only to hard choices for new researchers, but also to difficulties for those wishing to contrast or replicate results of previous work. Even when similar methods are chosen, the lack of controls makes comparison questionable. Investigations are often performed on widely different or rapidly evolving operating systems and user interfaces, and habits of user populations may be site-specific.

A second problem with natural studies of user interfaces is the difficulty of collecting data. Monitoring real life human–computer interaction is not easy. Source code may not be available for modification; interactions may go through a suite of programs rather than through a single one; security measures at the site may preclude close study. Furthermore, subjects may be hard to obtain. People resist conscription, perhaps due to concerns about privacy or plain inertia, or site populations are just too small for adequate sampling. Corporate reluctance also hinders data collection, for computer and human resources are expensive. Monitoring users takes processor time, physical records of user activities need substantial disk space, and subjects' time is costly.

With these provisos in mind, natural studies can, at least in principle, give valuable insight into people's behavior when using computers. One popular vehicle for such studies is UNIX.

2.1.2   A brief introduction to UNIX

UNIX is a widely used multitasking operating system that runs on a variety of computers, and is well described in many academic and popular publications (e.g., Ritchie and Thompson, 1974; Kernighan and Mashey, 1981; Pike and Kernighan, 1984; Waite, 1987). From the user's point of view, it has several important components. One is the file system, where all files are organized within hierarchical directories. Directories and files can be manipulated by users in all the standard ways. Users often work within the confines of a single "current" directory, although resources located in other directories are generally available as well.

Another important feature of UNIX is that no distinction is made between files containing programs and those containing other things (such as command scripts); any file is eligible for execution.[1] Although UNIX contains a large but standard repertory of programs, there is no difference between invoking a system program and a user program. This is significant because it allows one to tailor a system to individual needs simply by writing utility programs and putting them in the right place, without having to alter the innards of the system in any way. By setting search paths, users can tell UNIX to look for executable programs in specific directories

---

[1]Technically, an execution bit has to be set before a file can be run as a program. However, this bit can be easily set by a user with the appropriate permissions.

containing the standard system libraries, the user's own personal libraries, or files belonging to other members of the community. However, this flexibility has drawbacks. It encourages users to build and share extensive libraries of commands, causing difficulties with the naming of different programs and multiple versions of programs. Other users may come to rely on programs in a personal library without the owner's knowledge, in the erroneous belief that they were "standard" utilities (Witten and Greenberg, 1985).

The third UNIX component is its user interface, a command line interpreter called a *shell*[2] that comes in several flavors, the most popular in North America being *csh* (Joy, 1980). As with most conventional command-driven systems, *csh* is a passive slave awaiting orders; no attempt is made to guide or help the user. *Csh* implements incremental interaction. Once an order is received, it carries it out and then awaits the next command. Despite the proliferation of screen-based programs (especially editors), the basic *csh* interface is teletype-like. No use is made of the cursor control features provided by most VDUs. With the exceptions of the character-erase, word-erase, and line-erase capabilities, the screen is treated as a long roll of paper. Through the shell, users compose, edit, and then submit an input line to UNIX. The usual form of a submission is a command, optionally followed by an argument list.[3] Although the command may be handled directly by *csh*, it typically creates a new process by executing a file containing either compiled code produced by a programming language, or a script of further command lines. The argument list is made available to the program, and it can have two components: options and objects. Options modify the standard meaning of the program, that is, they "reshape" the tool. The program acts on the objects, which are usually UNIX file names or strings. Arguments may contain regular expressions (sometimes called wild cards) that are replaced by the shell with the names of files matching the expression.

Two other *csh* facilities are worth noting. With *history*, users may recall (rather than retype) part or all of a previously entered command line submission (see Section 4.1.1). With *aliases*, users may specify a name (the alias) and a definition. When the alias is typed on the command line, *csh* will substitute the definition in its place. Aliases allow users to redefine a command name, to customize commands by specifying default options, and to abbreviate a longer command line sequence.

UNIX users can tie together resources by redirecting input and output between programs, files, the keyboard, and the screen; this feature distinguishes UNIX from other command line systems. A standard UNIX program takes its input from the keyboard and places its output on the screen. Yet the same program can work with files, simply by using the two redirection symbols < and >, which stream input

---

[2]The command line interpreter is called a *shell* because it surrounds the kernel of the operating system (Quarterman, Silberschatz, and Peterson, 1985).

[3]Although *csh* contains a rudimentary programming language, it is rarely used at the command line level.

from file to program and output from program to file respectively. Program-to-program communication is supported through the pipe symbol |, eliminating the need for explicit temporary files. For example, consider the *sort* command that sorts its input lines, and the *uniq* command that removes succeeding copies of identical lines. Typed by itself, *sort* waits for a user to enter all the input lines through the keyboard, and prints the ordered results to the screen afterward. In the command line *sort* < *in* > *out*, the lines in the file *in* are sorted and then written to the new file *out*. Finally, the sequence *sort* < *in* | *uniq* uses the output of *sort* as the input to *uniq*; an ordered list of the unique lines contained in the file *in* is written to the screen. Through redirection and pipes, the user can "combine" UNIX tools.

Because no distinction is made between user and system software, and because input and output are easily passed between programs, UNIX works well when many small, general-purpose modules are available as building blocks for new programs. This follows from the cornerstone philosophy of UNIX:[4]

> Make each program do one thing well. To do a new job, build afresh rather than complicate old programs by adding "new" features. Expect the output of every program to become the input of another, as yet unknown program. ...Do not insist on interactive input.
> — McIlroy, Pinson, and Tague, 1978

The building blocks approach has drawbacks. Although small programs can be combined in many ways not anticipated by the original designer, it is sometimes hard to perform common operations without resorting to some level of rudimentary "programming." Less experienced users are often overwhelmed by the complexity of the system (Dzida, Hoffmann, and Valder, 1987). Still, it is the power and richness of UNIX that make it interesting. Because diverse utilities are available, and program creation and sharing are encouraged, UNIX fits the description of a general-purpose environment given in the last chapter.

2.1.3 Why study UNIX?

UNIX is a twenty-year-old operating system whose command line interface no longer represents current ideas in interface design.[5] Even at its best, the UNIX interface is full of well-known deficiencies (Norman, 1981). Then why study UNIX? Why not look at, say, a modern icon-based interface instead? This section

---

[4]Some people believe that current versions of UNIX have seriously compromised the "one tool one job" philosophy (Waite, 1987; Pike and Kernighan, 1984).

[5]UNIX was first developed in 1969 by Ken Thompson and the Computer Science Research Center of Bell Laboratories in Murray Hill. Originally written for the DEC PDP-7 computer and influenced by the Multics operating system, it was not publicly licensed and widely released until 1976 (Quarterman, Silberschatz, and Peterson, 1985).

argues that studying UNIX is indeed fruitful for several reasons: it is still in heavy use; it generalizes across many other systems; a body of knowledge of UNIX behavior currently exists; and finding and monitoring subjects is relatively straightforward.

Generalization. One attraction of UNIX is that it is not a contrived "toy" system. Rather, it is widely used, very powerful, and potentially complex, and has a broad range of users (Kraut, Hanson, and Farber, 1983). Because it is a general-purpose computing environment fulfilling many needs, any results garnered from it may generalize to other systems. In contrast, many high-performance graphical interfaces are so customized to particular applications that generalizations would be difficult to make and support.

Although direct-manipulation systems are becoming more popular, command line interfaces such as UNIX still pervade computer use. Some examples from mainframe and personal computing environments are VAX VMS, Honeywell Multics, APOLLO Domain, CPM, IBM VM, and IBM DOS. Hierarchical menus based on either text or graphics are usually little more than syntactic sugar placed on top of a command line system.[6] Observations made of UNIX usage probably apply to all these systems too.

If UNIX findings could not be generalized, they would still be valuable in their own right. Although old, UNIX is far from dying. Rather, it is being rapidly disseminated as a de facto open system standard on diverse machines, running the gamut from mainframes to workstations and personal computers. Even users of graphical direct-manipulation interfaces can thirst for UNIX, as illustrated by the availability of UNIX on the Apple Macintosh. Vendors have recently modernized UNIX by embedding it within a window environment. The SUN workstation, for example, has a suite of window-based front ends to popular UNIX facilities, including the shell, debugger, mail system, terminal emulator, directory browser, and so on (Sun, 1986b). More ambitiously, the developers of the NeXT machine have built a full-blown direct manipulation environment around the UNIX operating system (but users can still bring up the familiar shell in a glass teletype window).

An existing body of knowledge. Another appeal of UNIX to researchers is that it has already been studied extensively. There is probably more knowledge and raw data available on UNIX usage than any other computer system. The scientific process is more easily realized; other UNIX studies can be replicated, and previous findings can be built upon.

---

[6]MENUNIX, summarized in Chapter 8, is an example of a menu-based interface built directly on UNIX (Perlman, 1984).

Finding and monitoring subjects. A pragmatic advantage of studying UNIX is that it is relatively easy to do, because large groups of diverse people use it at many different sites. Although the system is generally perceived to be expert-oriented, there is no question that a significant number of non-programmers with widely varying needs also harness its power. UNIX is often the standard system employed by research institutions. The benevolent setting allows large-scale realistic studies that span user categories.

At the University of Calgary, for example, UNIX is used heavily in the Department of Computer Science by people with quite diverse programming skills and personal requirements. It is also available to people in several non-computer departments. The academic setting not only provides a captive audience, but also encourages participation – bureaucratic procedures are in place for conscripting subjects for study. Finally, UNIX source code for its programs are available for modification.

In summary, it is assumed that observed usage patterns of UNIX are fundamental to most computer-based imperative interactions. Methodological motivation arises from the number of diverse users, the relative ease of collecting data, and the existence of other findings for comparison. Studies of UNIX usage are generalizable, and have already affected the design of leading-edge systems. For example, Card and Henderson (1987) describe a multiple virtual workspace interface to support user task switching, motivated by the UNIX study of Bannon, Cypher, Greenspan, and Monty (1983) (see Sections 8.3 and 8.1).

2.2   Techniques for analyzing activities of UNIX users

As mentioned previously, many computer studies lack a standard methodology for data collection. UNIX studies are no exception, and records of interactions obtained range from low-level input traces collected over large user populations through to protocol analyses elicited from a few select subjects. This section surveys common methods that have been used for studying UNIX, and indicates their associated advantages and drawbacks.

2.2.1   Traces of user activity

A record of interactions between user and computer, usually collected through an unobtrusive software monitor, is called a *trace*. In natural studies of UNIX usage, voluminous amounts of data are often collected and sifted through in the hope that something interesting may turn up. Alternatively, a subject may be asked to solve particular problems, and his performance monitored over short-term tasks. This second approach is fruitful for testing hypotheses about user behavior and for exploring subdomains of UNIX. A measure of validity is obtained by comparing traces generated by the artificial task to those generated under normal circumstances

(Lewis, 1986).

The methods listed below describe ways that traces have been generated on UNIX.

Method 1: recording all keystrokes entered. Every single character entered on the command line is recorded, including the special line-editing characters (e.g., <backspace>) and non-alphanumeric characters (e.g., <return>). The monitoring software is fairly easy to write. In UNIX, for example, an interposed pseudo-tty filter can catch and note all keystrokes on entry before passing them on to the primary application. This easily implemented method supplies a complete record of all input. Yet there are several disadvantages. First, unnecessary data is collected. Unless the study is concerned with line editing or similar low-level artifacts, no benefit is gained by including such primitive operations. The final line, as seen by the user before a <return> is selected, would suffice for most purposes. Second, such traces are not easily read due to the inclusion of special editing characters. Consider, for example, the following input characters for a line taken from a typical script (Lewis, 1986), where $\wedge H$ represents a <backspace>, $\wedge M$ a return, and $\sqcup$ a space:

$$lsa \sqcup \wedge H \sqcup \wedge H \wedge H \sqcup \wedge H \wedge H \sqcup \wedge Hm - \wedge H \sqcup \wedge H \wedge H \sqcup \wedge Hs \sqcup -F \wedge M$$

After editing, the line translates to *ls* −*F*.[7] A third more serious disadvantage is that the *csh* manipulations of the line are not recorded. Once a line is entered, the *csh* expands wild cards, history substitutions, and aliases. Although the expanded line may reflect the intention of the user more closely, it is not captured by recording keystrokes only.

Method 2: session transcripts. A variant of recording keystrokes is recording complete transcripts of a login session, which includes the user's input and the system's response. Saving transcripts as a textual record is simple, for there is a standard UNIX facility to do so. No additional programming is necessary. If the interface follows a glass-teletype style of dialog, the record will be human readable as a sequential script. If the interface uses cursor control or graphical interaction, it is probably best to view the transcript as an animated playback record instead (not available in standard UNIX).

Transcripts are information rich, which is their weakness as well as their strength. Although they work well for small studies involving short sessions, the data pro-

---

[7]The number of keystrokes used to enter text is significantly more than the number of final characters. In a study of document creation through an editor, Whiteside, Archer, Wixon, and Good (1982) observed that only one-half of a user's keystrokes are for text entry. The rest were for cursor movement (1/4), text deletion (1/8), and so on.

duced for anything larger is so voluminous that it is almost impossible to handle. Transcripts are best used in pilot studies, or as a way of augmenting other data collection methods.

For example, Akin, Baykan, and Radha Rao (1987) performed a case study of the structure of the UNIX directory space by reviewing transcripts of users asked to carry out certain tasks. Even though only two subjects were used, and the task duration was limited to half an hour, they reported that the records were lengthy and hard to analyze. However, the transcripts did provide insight into user's movement in the directory space.

Method 3: recording lines expanded by *csh*. Instead of collecting data by catching keystrokes as they are entered, the complete line submitted can be captured as a chunk after it has been entered and processed by *csh*. All the noise produced by line editing would be removed. This is easily accomplished through the *csh* history facility, where lines automatically recorded by the system can be saved in a file. Desmarais and Pavel (1987), for example, collected and analyzed short-term UNIX traces by this method, and applied the information to generate user models.

Extra information known to *csh* can be trapped and noted as well by placing "hooks" within the *csh* program itself. In-line expansion of history use, aliases, and regular expressions can be recorded, as well as the current working directory of the user and the error status after execution is attempted. This is the method used in the current study, which will be described further in Section 2.3. The data collected is, of course, substantially richer than the data supplied by standard UNIX history. The catch is that modifying the source for *csh* is required. Because this contains over 16,000 lines of sparsely documented and quite complex code, the task is daunting.[8]

There are several problems with recording lines expanded by *csh*. First, not all user activity is captured. Although recording *csh* lines works well for "batch" style programs that execute and return without user intervention, it is not appropriate when highly interactive applications are used (e.g., editors). Interactive information is lost because data is collected from the *csh* command line only. Also, commands cannot be considered "equal." For example, consider a trace containing only two UNIX commands: *ls* for listing files; and *emacs*, which invokes a sophisticated interactive editor. Whereas file listing is accomplished almost immediately, an editing session can last for hours. This distinction is not captured by *csh*. A second disadvantage with this recording method is that the actual processes spawned by the command line are not noted. There are many ways to execute programs in UNIX: directly by name, indirectly through an alias or *csh* variable, or as a suite

---

[8]Four months were required to produce an acceptable tested version of *csh* that included a robust monitoring facility, even though the final number of modifications required was relatively small. This time includes the bureaucratic red tape involved with obtaining *csh* source.

of programs through a script. Because of this diversity, users can invoke the same program by many different names. For example, *e, emacs,* and *ed* may all invoke the same editor. Because only the text typed to *csh* is collected, the actual processes executed are left as an educated guess.

Tracing lines expanded by *csh* is a tradeoff between recording too much and too little information. By selectively combining this method with other ways of recording data, most problems noted above are correctable. For example, Lewis (1986) includes the final expanded line along with the command line as issued.

Method 4: recording processes spawned by user's commands. A popular method of analyzing UNIX usage exploits data collected by the standard system accounting packages, which records the processes spawned from a user's command rather than the command itself. The advantages lie in the ease of collecting data, and in having a record of the system's response to the user's activity. Unlike some previous methods, no program generation or modification is necessary.

But recording processes spawned is severely limited. First, many commands spawn multiple processes not mentioned explicitly by the user. Recording of processes reflects the user's command selection only when the generated process matches the submitted command, which is often not the case. A command may create multiple processes, and inferring what was actually typed by the user can be difficult. Researchers using this method have to develop strategies for eliminating the extra processes from the record. These include sifting the data by hand (Bannon and O'Malley, 1984), by a filter (Draper, 1984), or by supplementing the process data with command line data (Kraut, Hanson, and Farber, 1983).

Another major problem with recording processes only is the impoverished information produced. All options and arguments qualifying the command are lost, because the record indicates only the processes executed. Yet these are critical for understanding how a command is used. Also, commands handled directly by *csh* cannot be detected, as they do not spawn new processes (e.g., Draper, 1984). Furthermore, the use of aliases and history use is not noticed, because processes are created only after the line has been expanded.

A final problem stems from the difficulty of handling processes generated from user-written programs or scripts that are not part of the standard UNIX library. These are surely important, for UNIX encourages users to supplement system software with personal software. Yet some previous studies simply ignored those processes that were not within the system domain, usually by filtering out the unknown ones from the process list (Draper, 1984). Still, noting processes gives a reasonable approximation of the commands entered and executed by users.

2.2.2 Protocol analysis

Although some analysis of user activities is possible by studying traces, inferring a user's high-level intentions from a low-level record is always difficult. A better method of discovering intentions is to have users describe their activities as they are performed, a technique called *protocol analysis*. Some ways that protocol analysis has been used within UNIX are noted below.

Method 5: annotation of traces. Users are asked to annotate periodically a history list of commands with their intentions during a login session, perhaps by thinking aloud or by textual in-line comments. For example, Jorgensen (1987) instructed subjects to talk aloud while performing an artificial task involving UNIX mail. Their comments were recorded on audio tape and the important ones were later merged with transcript logs collected by the second method. Similarly, talking aloud into a tape recorder has been used in UNIX studies by Jennifer Jerrams-Smith.[9]

The example below gives a portion of a textually annotated trace, as recorded by Bannon, Cypher, Greenspan, and Monty (1983).

> *Write Info report. Its going to take a long time and be interrupted by other activities*
> 15 vi Ireport
>
> *Interrupted to prepare a memo. Send note to gm about outcome*
> 16 snd gm
>
> *Back to Ireport*
> 17 fg
> 18 lf HMI ...

Alternatively, the researcher may take a more active role and discuss the trace with the user either during or after the session (see method 7).

An objection to this form of protocol analysis is its obtrusiveness. Because of this, annotations are sometimes deferred until the end of an interactive session. Perhaps a more serious problem is that annotations may not reflect actual intentions. When comments are noted after a set of activities are performed, they may reflect post hoc rationalizations of actions rather than real situations (Suchman, 1987).

Method 6: constructive interaction. One way of removing the disruptive effect of annotations is through *constructive interaction*, where natural discussion between interacting participants of a study is used to reveal underlying processes (Miyake, 1982). When applied to studies of human–computer interaction, cooperating users are videotaped while solving a problem on a computer, although other resources may be made available to facilitate discussion. This is a good way of revealing the

---

[9] J. Jerrams-Smith, AI Group, Philips Research Laboratories, Redhill Surrey, UK.

users' mental model of particular concepts, especially when one or both participants are discussing a topic they do not fully understand (O'Malley, Draper, and Riley, 1984; Suchman, 1987).

In contrast to regular thinking aloud (fifth method), Jorgensen (1987) noted that sessions involving constructive interaction were "more lively, and that far more points were elicited spontaneously." He also suggested that subjects were encouraged to continue their tasks by the presence of their colleagues. On the down side, he reported that the mixing of two individual lines of thought into one sometimes produced a confusing picture of events.

Method 7: interviews and questionnaires. A simple method of eliciting knowledge about the high-level intentions of a user is through questions asked before or after the user performs a task.[10] A group of users may be queried on paper (questionnaires) or verbally (interviews) for their views on the system. For example, Sutcliffe and Old (1987) used a questionnaire to elicit preliminary information on user experiences, attitudes, and knowledge with UNIX, and the typical tasks performed. Command traces were then logged through the fourth method described in the previous subsection. These were annotated in a set of follow-up interviews where users were asked to verbalize their recorded task sequences. Sutcliffe and Old mention that system logs proved the most valuable of the three methods.

2.3 Data collection for the current study

In this study, command line data was collected from users of the UNIX *csh* command interpreter. The selection and grouping of subjects, and the method of data collection, are described in this section.

Subjects. The subjects were 168 unpaid volunteers. All were either students or employees of the University of Calgary.

Subject use. Four target groups were identified, representing a total of 168 male and female users with a wide cross-section of computer experience and needs. Salient features of each group are described below, while the sample sizes (the number of people observed) are indicated in Table 2.1.

> *Novice Programmers.* Conscripted from an introductory Pascal course, these subjects had little or no previous exposure to programming, operating systems, or UNIX-like command-based interfaces. Such subjects spent most of their computer time learning how to program and use the basic system facilities.

---

[10]Because they are not performed during the task, interviews and questionnaires are not, strictly speaking, methods of protocol analysis.

Table 2.1. *Sample group sizes and statistics of the command lines recorded*

Name	Sample size	Total number of command lines	Number of command lines excluding errors		
			total	mean	std dev
Novice Programmers	55	77,423	73,288	1,333	819.8
Experienced Programmers	36	74,906	70,234	1,950	1,276.0
Computer Scientists	52	125,691	119,557	2,299	2,022.9
Non-programmers	25	25,608	24,657	986	1,155.6
Total	168	303,628	287,736	1,712	1,498.8

Experienced Programmers. Members were senior computer science undergraduates who were expected to have a fair knowledge of programming languages and the UNIX environment. As well as coding, word processing, and employing more advanced UNIX facilities to fulfill course requirements, these subjects used the system for social and exploratory purposes.

Computer Scientists. This group, comprised of faculty, graduates, and researchers from the Department of Computer Science, had varying experience with UNIX, although all were experts with computers in general. Tasks performed were less predictable and more varied than other groups, spanning advanced program development, research investigations, social communication, maintaining databases, word processing, satisfying personal requirements, and so on.

Non-programmers. Word processing and document preparation was the dominant activity of this group, made up of office staff and members of the Faculty of Environmental Design. Little program development occurred – tasks were usually performed with existing application packages. Knowledge of UNIX was the minimum necessary to get the job done.

Because users were assigned to subject groups only through their membership in identifiable user groups (e.g., computer science graduate students), their placement in these categories cannot be considered strictly rigorous. Although it was assumed that they generally follow their group stereotype, uniform behavior was not expected.

Instructions to subjects. As part of the solicitation process, subjects were informed verbally or by letter that:

- data on their normal UNIX use would be monitored and collected at the command line level only;

- the data collected would be kept confidential;
- any public reference or dissemination of the data and derived results would guarantee anonymity, unless explicit permission was given by the subject to do otherwise;
- at any time during the study period the subject could request that data collection stop immediately;
- there would be no noticeable degrading of system performance;
- if requested, data collected from a subject would be made available to him or her.

These subjects did not require nor did they receive any additional instructions during the actual study period. No subject asked to be withdrawn from the experiment, and no one asked to see their personal data.[11]

Apparatus. A modified *csh* was installed on three VAX 11/780s located in the Department of Computer Science and one VAX 11/750 in the Faculty of Environmental Design, all within the University of Calgary. Many different terminals were available to participants, most which were traditional character-based VDUs. In addition, CORVUS CONCEPT workstations running the JADE window manager were available to members of the Experienced and Computer Scientist groups (Greenberg, Peterson, and Witten, 1986). As with many window systems, this workstation allowed users to create many "virtual terminal" windows, each running *csh*, on a single screen.

Method. Command line data was collected continuously for the four months between February 1987 and June 1987 from users of a modified Berkeley 4.2 UNIX *csh* command interpreter (Joy, 1980). From the user's point of view, monitoring was unobtrusive – the modified command interpreter was identical in all visible respects to the standard version. The total number of command lines recorded per group is listed in Table 2.1.

Data was collected by the third method of Section 2.2.1 – recording lines expanded by *csh*. Table 2.2 lists the trace information annotated by the modified *csh*. Login sessions are distinguished by a record that notes the start and end time of each session (the 'S' and 'E' fields in the table). Command lines entered during this period are then listed in following records, each annotated with the current working directory, alias substitution (if any), history use, and error status. The final command line accepted by *csh*, including history expansions and ignoring editing operations that form the line, is recorded in the "C" field. The "D" field notes the directory that the user was in when the command line was entered. The

---

[11] See Appendix A in Greenberg (1988a) for a copy of a typical information sheet provided to subjects.

Table 2.2. *Trace information annotated by the modified* csh

Code	Description	Example
	Login session record	
S	Start time of the login session	S Fri Feb 6 15:54:25 1987
E	End time of the login session	E Fri Feb 6 17:25:01 1987
	Command line record	
C	The line entered by the user	C ls –a
D	The current working directory	D /user/greenberg/bin
A	The alias expansion of the previous command (if any)	A ls –a
H	The line entered had a history expansion in it (True or Nil)	H True
X	The error detected in the line by *csh* (if any). A following letter and number code indicates the category and actual error type.	X N 10

alias expansion of the line is found in the "A" field, whereas the "H" field indicates whether or not *csh* history helped form the line. System errors generated by *csh* are registered in the "X" field. Although eleven categories and many sub-categories of errors are annotated, the distinctions between them are not used in the current study. The total and average number of command lines collected excluding these errors are listed in Table 2.1

An example trace is given in Appendix A. Appendix B provides summary statistics for each subject, including the number of login sessions, the command lines entered, the different commands used, the *csh* errors noted, the times history was used, and the different directories accessed.

Data selection. If subjects did not log in at least 10 times and execute at least 100 commands during the study period, their data was not considered. By these criteria, 12 of the 180 original participants were rejected. Particular manipulations of the data, the analyses performed, and the results obtained are described in later chapters.

Motivation. Participants used UNIX as usual. Users were neither encouraged nor expected to alter their everyday use of the system. As subjects had few reminders that their command line interactions were being traced, they were largely oblivious to the monitoring process.

Availability of data. All data collected is available to – and has been used by – other researchers. A research report describes its format, and includes a cartridge tape of the data (Greenberg, 1988b). The report and data are available from the Department of Computer Science, University of Calgary, or the author. To ensure the confidentiality promised above, data was massaged to remove the identity of subjects.

Problems. Because of implementation difficulties, the details of history directives are not recorded. The altered *csh* indicates only that history has been used, and notes the command line retrieved through history. It does not record the actual history directive used to produce the modification.

2.4 Concluding remarks

This chapter argued that it is worthwhile to study data collected from everyday use of UNIX. Previous methodologies used for capturing UNIX interactions were examined, and the particulars of the method employed by the current investigation were listed.

One difficulty of studying and analyzing UNIX comes not from considerations of methodology, but from personal biases of the scientific and user communities. Because UNIX is so popular, and because reports of its deficiencies (and corresponding remedies) are so numerous, it is perceived by some to be a "straw man" that is easily picked upon. A reaction to yet another UNIX study could be apathy. Yet all UNIX investigations are not alike. The main purpose of this study, like a handful of others, is not to improve UNIX – it is too late for that. Rather, I assume that UNIX investigations are best harnessed to illuminate fundamental properties of human behavior when using similar general-purpose environments. If doubts exist about generalization, the methodology may be applied to other systems for empirical comparisons.

This study could have been performed on almost any other system with a rich set of constructs. UNIX *csh* was chosen for pragmatic considerations, and because I believe its usage reflects that of other systems.

3

Using commands in UNIX

This chapter examines how people use commands in command-based systems.[1] Like previous work, it is based on an analysis of long-term records of user–computer interaction with the UNIX *csh* command interpreter, collected as described in the previous chapter. The results of the major studies are reevaluated, particularly those of Hanson, Kraut, and Farber (1984), and Draper (1984), and some of the work is replicated. Although the statistical results of the studies are supported, some of the conclusions made by the original researchers are found to be misleading.

The following sections provide details of how people direct command-based systems in terms of how individual commands are selected and the dependencies between these commands. It is essential to take into account the fact that pooled statistics may conceal important differences between individuals. As a consequence, the results are analyzed by user and by identifying groups of similar users, as well as by pooling data for the entire population.

For the current study, a *command* is the first word entered in the command line. Those lines that produced system errors were not considered. The first word is parsed by removing all white space at the beginning of the line and counting all characters up to but not including the next white space or end of line. For example, the command parsed from the command line

$$\text{print } -f \ 31 \ -t \ 40 \ \text{galley.text}$$

is "print." The parsed word is almost always a true UNIX command or alias that invokes a program or shell script. This method does not record all the UNIX commands used, for an input line may contain more than one command (e.g., by redirecting input and output with pipes, or by cascading separate command sequences). Still, it seems a reasonable approximation.

3.1 Frequency distributions of commands for large groups

Several investigators have examined the frequency of command usage by a user population (Peachey, Bunt, and Colbourn, 1982; Kraut, Hanson, and Farber, 1983; Hanson, Kraut, and Farber, 1984; Ellis and Hitchcock, 1986). All studies report results approximated by a Zipf distribution, which has the property that a

---

[1]Some of the findings in this chapter were first presented at the 3rd IFAC Conference on Man–Machine Systems, Oulu, Finland (Greenberg and Witten, 1988a).

relatively small number of items have high usage frequencies, and a very large number of items have low usage frequencies (Zipf, 1949; Witten, Cleary, and Greenberg, 1984).

A looser characteristic of this kind of rank distribution is the well-known 80–20 rule of thumb that has been commonly observed in commercial transaction systems – 20% of the items in question are used 80% of the time (Knuth, 1973; Peachey, Bunt, and Colbourn, 1982).[2] In measurements recorded from a UNIX site, Hanson, Kraut, and Farber (1984) report a similar trend – 10% of the 400–500 commands available account for 90% of the usage. These models also hold for the frequency distribution of all help requests made for particular commands through the UNIX on-line manual[3] (summarized in Section 5.3.1; also see Greenberg, 1984).

The current study supports these observations. Figure 3.1 illustrates the command frequency distribution for each of the four different user groups described in the previous chapter. The frequency distribution is not a probability distribution. It gives the relative frequency between commands, rather than the actual frequency of use. The vertical axis shows the number of command invocations, normalized to one for the most frequent, whereas the horizontal axis shows the rank ordering of commands, with the most frequent first. Only the twenty highest ranking commands for each group are shown. For example, the most frequently selected command by the Experienced Programmer group is positioned first in the rank order, and is used at a relative frequency of 1. The second most selected (rank order of two) is used at a relative frequency of 0.94, the third at 0.49, the fourth at 0.35, and so on down the list. The Zipf curve, normalized in the same way and calculated as $y = x^{-1}$, is illustrated by the smooth line in the figure, and seems to provide a plausible model for the observed frequencies. For each of the four user groups, 10% of the commands used accounted for 84%–91% of all usage (cf Hanson's 10%–90%).[4] This ratio seems independent of both the actual number of different commands used by a group and the size of the sample group.

3.2 Usage frequency of particular commands between groups

Even though frequency statistics of different groups are modeled by the Zipf distribution, it is worth asking whether commands retain the same rank order between different user groups. If they do, then a command used frequently by one group will have the same relative usage in another. As will be seen later in this chapter, this is not necessarily the case.

---

[2]This rule is recursive, as the 80–20 rule also applies to the most active 20% (Knuth, 1973).

[3]Every command in the UNIX system usually has a corresponding manual entry, invoked by typing *man* <*command*>.

[4]Although similar results seem to apply to the top 10% of the command set, the recursive property of the rule cannot be checked reliably. Limits are quickly reached over the relatively small number of remaining commands.

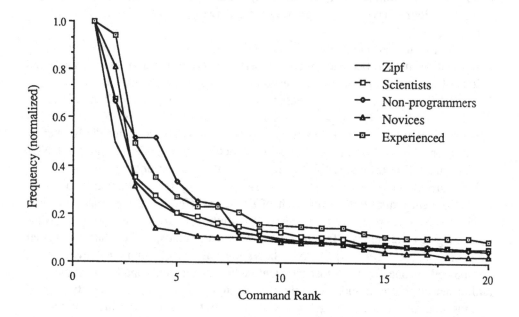

Figure 3.1. The normalized command frequency, compared with Zipf.

Table 3.1 gives the data from which Figure 3.1 is drawn.   Each column shows the twenty most frequently used commands by each group (including data reported by Hanson, Kraut, and Farber, 1984) and also provides the total number of commands executed, the number of different commands executed, and the number of users sampled. The few common high-frequency commands across the five user groups are mostly concerned with navigating, manipulating, and finding information about the file store (such as *ls, rm,* and *cd*). Comparison of other commands captures the differences between the groups. The emphasis on programming by both our novice and experienced subjects is reflected by the various compilers used (*pix* and *pi* for Pascal, *make* for "C," and *ada*). The non-programmers, on the other hand, seem concerned with word processing (as indicated by the relatively heavy use of *nroff* and *spell*). The type of editor also indicates group differences – *vi* and *ed* are chosen by Hanson's group, whereas *emacs, e, umacs, fred,* and *ed* have varying degrees of use within the others.

Grouping all subjects into one category also illustrates the danger of using a population stereotype to approximate the activity in each group. As shown by column 1 of Table 3.1, which pools all subjects of this study into one large sample, some high-frequency commands are not used frequently (if at all) by all groups (e.g., *pix, umacs*).

Table 3.1. *Command distributions of the top twenty commands for five different user groups*

		Groups from the current study								Others Hanson's group	
All subjects		Novice Programmers		Experienced Programmers		Computer Scientists		Non-programmers			
command	% used	command	% used	command	% used	command	% used	command	% used	command	% used
ls	13.33	pix	25.64	ls	12.76	ls	15.75	ls	18.53	cd	12.30
cd	8.83	umacs	20.89	cd	12.03	cd	10.62	emacs	12.35	ls	10.0
pix	6.69	ls	8.18	e	6.29	e	5.58	cd	9.56	cat	9.6
umacs	5.34	rm	3.55	fg	4.42	fg	4.32	nroff	9.55	|	6.2
e	4.47	u	3.19	more	3.49	rm	3.21	e	6.20	vi	5.9
rm	3.35	cat	2.79	make	2.93	mail	3.00	rm	4.66	ed	5.6
emacs	3.28	more	2.63	rm	2.93	emacs	2.58	ee	4.47	rm	3.8
fg	3.07	cd	2.61	emacs	2.66	lpq	2.36	lpq	2.25	;	2.7
more	2.51	script	2.49	l	2.02	more	2.06	ps	2.13	>	2.5
lpq	2.02	lpr	2.26	cat	1.96	ps	1.97	cp	1.66	Mail	2.0
mail	1.95	cp	2.09	lpr	1.91	f	1.70	proff	1.65	nroff	1.5
cat	1.89	lpq	2.08	ada	1.85	cat	1.62	more	1.59	mail	2.0
lpr	1.49	emacs	1.95	ex-vax	1.85	who	1.59	w	1.50	mv	1.2
cp	1.48	pi	1.54	cp	1.58	mv	1.20	mail	1.37	grep	1.2
ps	1.36	p	1.21	rwho	1.37	man	1.18	rr	1.31	col	0.9
who	1.14	fred	1.04	a.out	1.33	rlogin	1.05	tbl	1.27	echo	0.9
make	1.08	mail	1.03	mail	1.31	cp	1.02	spell	1.27	&	0.9
nroff	1.06	pdpas	0.72	lpq	1.31	fred	0.99	mv	1.20	tail	0.7
fred	0.95	logout	0.71	ps	1.30	lpr	0.91	ed	1.02	pwd	0.7
man	0.90	pdp60	0.67	who	1.16	page	0.90	apq	0.89	awk	0.7
Commands executed											
287,736		73,288		70,234		119,557		24,657		9,934	
Different commands											
1,307		264		588		851		196		400	
Sample size											
168		55		36		52		25		16	

Even though the Zipf form of the frequency distribution remains intact between different groups of a population (Figure 3.1), the rank order of commands is not, in general, maintained.

3.3 Frequency distributions and command overlap between individuals

The extent to which the usage statistics of an individual resemble those of a group of like people is considered next. Does the Zipf distribution characterize each user's command interactions, or is it just an artifact of data grouping? Do individuals within a group invoke the same set of commands? One might expect the variation between users to be even greater than that between groups.

In the previously mentioned study of the UNIX on-line manual, the frequency distribution of help requests was analyzed between individuals (Greenberg, 1984). In general, users constrained themselves to relatively small subsets of the requests possible – they never accessed a great many potential entries. Moreover, when users' subsets were compared, the intersection between their elements was small and the frequency of access of the common elements varied considerably across users. Greenberg (1984) suggested that although individual help requests seem to follow the Zipf distribution in broad outline (but not in detail), it is not possible to make anything but the grossest generalization from a population perspective of how individual users will access particular items within a system. This study is summarized further in Section 5.3.1.

The same is true for command line interactions. While studying the nature of expertise in UNIX, Draper (1984) estimated the times a command was invoked by noting the UNIX processes spawned during each user's interaction with the system (method 4, Section 2.2.1).[5] He suggested that the overall trends observed are representative of real command use. First, out of a vocabulary of the 570 commands available to the population, only 394 (70%) were used at least once. Individuals knew the system to varying degrees – there was a fairly smooth distribution of vocabulary size up to the maximum of 236 commands known to one user. Characteristics of the overlap between individuals' vocabularies were similar to those found in Greenberg's (1984) study of the UNIX on-line manual. Generally, very few of each individual's commands were used by all the population, a few more were shared to some degree by other users, and the rest used by each individual alone. Draper concluded that vocabulary is a poor measure of expertise, and that each user is actually a specialist in a particular corner of the system.

Sutcliffe and Old (1987) pursued the matter further in a similar study by ranking commands by popularity. They established that the top twenty commands accounted for 73% of the overall number recorded. The remaining 27% accounted

---

[5]Sutcliffe and Old (1987) employed the same method to replicate portions of Draper's work. Their findings are similar throughout.

Table 3.2. *Number of users per command*

% of users sharing a command	Proportional number of commands shared (%)					
	All subjects	Novice Prog'rs	Exper'd Prog'rs	Computer Scientists	Non-prog'rs	Draper's group
100–91	0.2	2.7	2.2	0.9	1.5	0.5
90–81	0.3	0.8	0.7	0.8	0	2.0
80–71	0.3	0.4	1.0	0.8	2.0	3.1
70–61	0.4	0.8	1.0	0.6	0.5	3.3
60–51	0.5	1.5	2.2	1.9	4.6	3.1
50–41	0.5	2.7	1.9	1.1	3.1	6.1
40–31	1.2	0	1.2	1.4	4.6	6.1
30–21	1.5	9.1	4.1	4.4	6.6	8.6
20–11	3.0	12.1	8.9	6.5	34.7	17.8
10–0	92.0	70.1	76.9	81.7	42.4	49.5
Not shared						
	68.8	55.3	58.5	63.1	42.3	unknown
Total number of unique commands						
	1307	264	588	851	196	394
Mean number of unique commands per subject and standard deviation						
mean	50.3	27.8	66.4	72.1	29.6	unknown
std dev	32.5	18.0	24.9	32.7	20.1	unknown

for 236 further commands. However, these results may be misleading, for heavy use of a command by an individual will skew the distribution.

Even though Draper's method of data collection differed, this study corroborates his conclusions that users tend to know a particular corner of the system with very little overlap between them. The first ten rows of Table 3.2 show the proportion of commands shared by the users comprising a particular group. The following rows show the proportion of commands that are not shared, the total number of different commands entered by each group, and the average number of different commands per user. Table 3.3 lists the twenty most shared commands for each user group. For example, only 0.2% (i.e., 3) of the 1,307 different commands used by all subjects were shared by more than 90% of them (these were basic file manipulation commands for listing, removing, and copying files, as shown in column 1 of Table 3.3). More surprisingly, a full 92% of all shared commands were shared by fewer than 10% of the users, and 68.8% of the total command set seen are not shared at all. These differences are much stronger than those suggested by Draper's group (the last column of Table 3.2), probably because of inaccuracies in his methodology of estimating command use.

Tables 3.2 and 3.3 also reveal that categorizing like subjects into groups changes

Table 3.3. *The twenty most shared commands for each user group*

All subjects		Novice Programmers		Experienced Programmers		Computer Scientists		Non-programmers	
command	# of users	command	# of users	command	# of users	command	# of users	command	# of users
ls	168	lpr	55	cd	36	ls	52	ls	25
rm	164	ls	55	ls	36	rm	51	rm	24
cp	154	pix	55	more	36	cat	50	emacs	23
lpq	149	rm	55	lpq	35	cd	50	cd	19
lpr	144	script	55	man	35	mv	49	cp	19
cd	141	cp	53	cat	34	cp	48	nroff	18
cat	140	lpq	53	cp	34	mail	48	lpq	17
mail	131	umacs	47	lpr	34	man	48	ps	16
more	130	cat	46	mail	34	mkdir	46	lpr	14
man	124	more	42	mkdir	34	ftp	44	more	14
who	117	cd	36	rm	34	lpq	44	logout	13
mv	114	mail	36	ftp	33	ps	44	mail	13
emacs	112	limits	32	ps	32	pwd	44	man	13
mkdir	104	who	30	mv	31	who	44	hpq	12
ps	103	man	28	who	31	fg	42	mv	12
fg	95	pi	28	ruptime	30	e	41	spell	12
script	95	logout	26	fg	29	emacs	41	who	12
pwd	92	help	24	kill	28	lpr	41	kill	11
ftp	91	lquota	23	limits	28	rlogin	40	pwd	11
logout	88	emacs	23	rwho	28	kill	38	cat	10
Sample size									
	168		55		36		52		25

the figures less than one might expect. For example, even though individuals in the novice group used the system for solving the same programming assignments and were taught UNIX together, there was relatively little intersection of their vocabularies. Except for a handful of commands, users – even those with apparently similar task requirements and expertise – have surprisingly little vocabulary overlap.

3.4 Growth of the command vocabulary

In the previous discussion, a user's vocabulary was taken to be the set of commands invoked over a fixed period of time. But how dynamic is the command vocabulary of a user? Do users learn new commands sporadically or uniformly over time? Are new commands acquired continually, or do users stop acquiring new vocabulary after some initial period?

Sutcliffe and Old (1987) suggest that the size of a user's command set grows

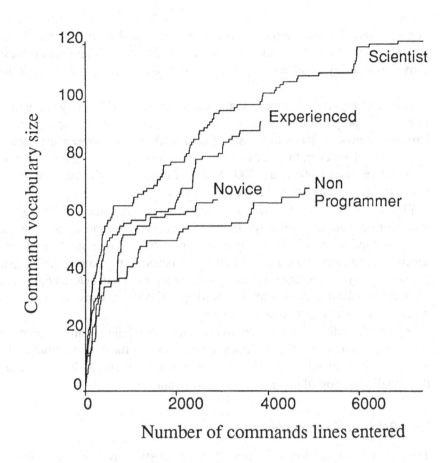

Figure 3.2. Command vocabulary size vs. the number of command lines entered for four individuals.

as a function of system usage. They found a significant correlation between the overall command use by the user and the number of unique commands employed. This evidence is suggestive but does not actually observe vocabulary acquisition by particular users. Figure 3.2, on the other hand, illustrates the acquisition of vocabulary over time for four typical users from the current study, with one from each group. The vertical axis is vocabulary size, whereas the horizontal axis represents the number of command lines entered so far. At first, the vocabulary growth rate seems to be around 5% – each user shown here has a repertoire of 43–64 commands after 1,000 full command lines had been entered. But the growth rate drops quickly afterward to 1% or less. The later part of the curve is probably a better reflection of vocabulary acquisition, for the first part does not necessarily reflect a learning curve. Because users already knew a command subset before monitoring began, unusually high initial activity is expected as known commands are being noticed for the first time. Another explanation is that the curve just represents the arrival probability of infrequent commands whose distribution patterns follow Zipf.

Although Figure 3.2 suggests that the selected subjects have a vocabulary growth rate that is proportional to the relative sophistication of the group, analysis of variance shows no statistically significant differences between the mean rate of each group. However, these rates were determined by counting the new commands acquired between 1,000 and 2,000 command entries, which meant excluding those subjects who did not have at least 2,000 entries.

Figure 3.2 also reveals how users acquire new commands. Although there are short periods where vocabulary growth is relatively uniform, there are also long periods of quiescence followed by a flurry of activity. As might be expected, these flurries were sometimes associated with new tasks. For example, the sharp increase in new activity for the Scientist group subject after she had entered 6,000 command lines all involved high-quality typesetting. However, there are other instances where no such task association is evident.

In general, individuals have small command vocabularies and acquire new ones slowly and irregularly. Given the patterns observed, the Zipf distribution becomes a questionable model of individual command use. Perhaps all that can be said is that the distribution of command use is very uneven.

3.5   Relations in command sequences

The previous discussion says nothing about possible relations and dependencies between commands. Through a multivariate analysis of UNIX commands invoked by the site population, Hanson, Kraut, and Farber (1984) examined the interaction effects between commands. Their results show statistically significant relationships between certain command chains; the relations between the fifty most frequently used commands are shown in Figure 3.3. Each ball in the network represents a command, its size indicates the usage frequency, and the arrow indicates the significant dependencies. One dimension of these relationships is *modularity*. Some commands, such as *ls*, are core commands – they are used frequently and are surrounded by many other commands (i.e., highly modular and independent). Others are not; they are surrounded by specific command sequences. An example of the latter is *cp*, which is generally preceded by itself and followed by *chmod*.

Commands are also related by functional clusters, such as editing, process management, orientation, social communication, and so on (Hanson, Kraut, and Farber, 1984), which may not be revealed by statistics. Consider a user who prints files in several ways: a short draft may go to the screen; a long listing to a lineprinter; and a final version to a laser printer. Although these non-sequential and possibly rarely invoked actions are related by function in the user's mind, it is unlikely that

UNIX COMMAND SEQUENCES

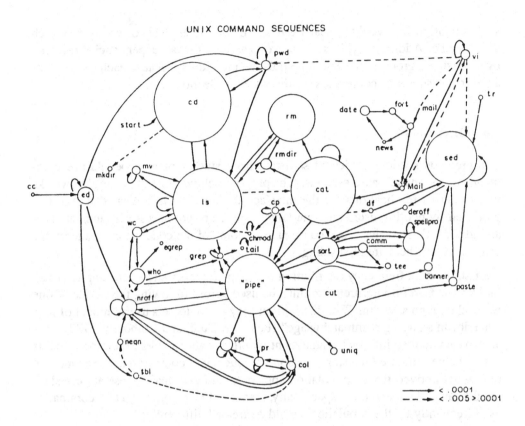

Ball diameters are proportional to stationary probability. Lines indicate significant dependencies, solid ones being more probable ($p < .0001$) and dashed ones less probable ($.005 < p < .0001$).

Figure 3.3. Sequential structure of UNIX command usage, from Figure 4 in Hanson et al. (1984).

such a relationship would appear from a multivariate analysis of commands such as Hanson's. Additionally, it is a mistake to assume that all dependencies revealed by analysing a group of users will hold for an individual, because each person uses a particular subset of commands (as discussed in Section 3.3).

3.6 Discussion

The previous sections reviewed statistics from studies of how people use commands in command-based systems. The purpose behind most of the original works was to derive implications for the interface design. Yet it is clear that statistics produced by pooling users into one large sample are not necessarily indicative of an individual's statistics. As a consequence, some of the conclusions made by the original researchers are misleading.

First, the rank frequency distribution of a population should not be applied to an individual. Careful interpretation must be used before following the advice of one researcher, who says "the Zipf distribution may prove to be a useful model of user behavior in studying command usage" (Peachey, Bunt, and Colbourn, 1982). It is all too easy to read into such a statement two implications. First, the Zipf model is a reasonable estimate for a single person's frequency of command use. Second, the rank order derived from a population applies to an individual. These are certainly not the case. Next, and more specifically, Hanson et al. recommend that commands used frequently by the population should be treated differently:

> the uneven distribution of command use suggests that computer systems should find ways to increase the prominence and ease of access to frequently used commands.
> — Hanson, Kraut, and Farber, 1984

Given the results of the previous sections, this should more correctly read "to increase the prominence and ease of access to an *individual's* frequently used commands." The slight wording difference is crucial. Whereas the original conclusion implies that command prominence may be judged and treated generically, the corrected version would require a personalized approach.

Second, it is a mistake to assume that users have similar vocabularies. Hanson et al. went on to say that computer systems should be organized with sets of frequently used core commands, implying that these sets are reasonably large and that core commands are shared. But the findings detailed in Section 3.3 refute this prescription in two ways. First, individuals have very few common commands. Second, people may use different resources for implementing those few actions that they have in common, for example, different editors and compilers for text processing and programming respectively. Sutcliffe and Old explain these phenomena.

Considering UNIX is a system rich in functionality but relatively unstructured, it is not surprising [that] users have created a variety of tasks with the tools available ... great creativity is exercised in implementing a rich diversity of tasks.
— Sutcliffe and Old, 1987

Perhaps the few shared and frequently used commands could best be handled as exceptions, possibly by bundling them into a finely tuned application. For example, the extremely heavy use by all users of the basic file manipulation commands, as noted in Tables 3.1 and 3.3, suggests that users require not only constant feedback on the contents of the current directory, but some simple tools for manipulating them as well. Feedback can be provided by keeping a permanent display of the current files on view, a simple task given a window-based environment. If screen real estate is a concern, transient windows popped up by a mouse press may be used instead (Greenberg, Peterson, and Witten, 1986). These findings also support the inclusion of the more sophisticated file browsers that are found in many modern programming environments.

Third, the relations between commands seen by Hanson's pooled statistics do not necessarily apply to individuals (Section 3.5). The dependencies and clustering observed may result from a small handful of people using a set of related commands frequently, and not from common use of the same commands by every person. Consider the recent findings of Sutcliffe and Old (1987). They replicated and extended Hanson's work by eliminating all dependencies but those that were significant for at least five or more individual users (cf. Figure 3.3). The resulting network was a fragmented subset of the population network. Sutcliffe and Old concluded that only a small number of commands were used in common tasks by a majority of individuals. Hanson, then, has insufficient evidence to suggest that

it would be practical to organize the commands around task-related menus. Commands that are likely to be used in one context may also be needed in others.
— Hanson, Kraut, and Farber, 1984

To their credit, Hanson et al. also state that such menus are best viewed as default organizations that, because of individual differences, should be customizable by the user.

In another area, many intelligent tutoring systems and the models they employ are motivated by possibly incorrect assumptions of command usage. Consider Hecking (1987), for example, who quotes the statistic "people use only 40% of all UNIX functions" (cf. Draper's 70%, Section 3.3). He claims that this situation is a poor one and advocates intelligent help systems as a remedy. Yet Draper (1984) contradicts this claim by suggesting that users are best viewed as specialists in their own corner of the system. Next, consider how expertise models are formed. One approach for deciding what knowledge should be presented to the user employs an "expert" and a "student" model (Sleeman and Brown, 1982). For example, the *differential* model of Burton and Brown (1982) bases its instructional presentation on the differences between a student's and an expert's behavior, and has been advocated in the UNIX domain (Chin, 1986). Desmarais and Pavel (1987) use a similar model to generate knowledge structures of commands. These structures indicate the likelihood that an observed command has been mastered by a person, and are used to infer what other commands he might know. Another expertise-based strategy is employed by the well-known UNIX Consultant, which stereotypes users into one of four levels of expertise and tailors its advice to them accordingly (Chin, 1986). But the above approaches are ill founded. Experienced users of general-purpose environments such as UNIX do not share particular command sets. Except for the very few common commands, it is not possible to decide what commands should be offered to the student. Consequently, the differential model is not necessarily appropriate for teaching people how to use general-purpose computer systems.

3.7   Concluding remarks

This chapter has surveyed and replicated studies in several areas involving user interactions with command-based computer systems. The trends observed are presumed to be shared by most command-based interactions; they are not just artifacts of the UNIX implementation. The major findings follow.

1. The rank frequency distribution of command usage by groups of like and unlike users is approximated by a Zipf distribution.
2. With a few exceptions, the frequency of use of most commands differs between groups – rank order is not maintained.
3. There is little overlap between the command vocabulary of different users, even for those with apparently similar task requirements and expertise.
4. Individuals have small command vocabularies, and new commands are acquired slowly and irregularly. Consequently, the Zipf model may not be an accurate estimate of an individual's behavior.
5. Some commands cluster around or follow others in statistically significant ways, although these dependencies vary from one individual to another.

These conclusions tell us more about individual differences than about similarities, and they are not as useful as one might hope. Although they do refute some previously held beliefs, the conclusions do not suggest any general new directions in interface design.

I believe that these studies place undue attention on command usage. The reductionist approach may have been pushed too far. Commands, after all, are only the verbs of the command line. They also act on objects, are qualified with options, and may redirect input and output to other commands. These other facets are surely important and should not be ignored. For example, UNIX lines sharing the same initial command may have completely different meanings. Consider the two command lines *sort file* and *sort file | uniq −c | sort −r*. The first just sorts a file, whereas the second produces a frequency count of the identical lines in the file. Another problem is that the same command line may satisfy rather different intentions. Ross, Jones, and Millington (1985) give an example of one person invoking the UNIX command line *ls −l* to distinguish between ordinary files and directories, whereas another person could use the same sequence to discover file creation dates and sizes. Accordingly, the UNIX usage data, analyzed in this chapter in terms of commands, is reanalyzed in Chapter 5 in terms of command lines.

How does all this fit into tool use, the theme of Chapter 1? If only commands are considered to be tools, then the tool set chosen by each user does not seem particularly rich. Few are selected, and of these only a handful are used to any great extent. Alternatively, if commands are viewed as simple building blocks used to manufacture more sophisticated or specialized tools – perhaps by reshaping (setting options), combining them (redirection, pipelines, and sequencing), or by varying the objects they deal with – then every unique command line entered can be considered a new tool. The latter view is advocated in the remaining chapters.

I will argue that, as with tools, the work environment should support and enhance the way people use complete command lines. Recently used submissions should be available for reuse, and people should be able to organize their command lines by function and by task. The next four chapters of the book consider the first strategy – reuse. Afterward, Chapter 8 considers the ways people organize their activities, and Chapter 9 describes an implemented design of a user support tool that allows people to reuse and store command lines (as they do tools) through a workbench metaphor.

4

Techniques for reusing activities

Those who ignore history are destined to retype it
—Ben Shneiderman

It is evident that users often repeat activities they have previously submitted to the computer. These activities include not only the commands they choose from the many available in command-driven systems (Chapter 3), but also the complete command line entry. Similarly, people repeat the ways they traverse paths within menu hierarchies, select icons within graphical interfaces, and choose documents within hypertext systems. Often, recalling the original activity is difficult or tedious. For example, problem-solving processes must be recreated for complex activities; command syntax or search paths in hierarchies must be remembered; input lines retyped; icons found; and so on. Given these difficulties, potential exists for a well-designed "reuse facility" to reduce the problems of activity reformulation.

But most system interfaces offer little support for reviewing and reusing previous activities. Typically they must be completely retyped, or perhaps reselected through menu navigation. Those systems that do provide assistance offer ad hoc "history" mechanisms that employ a variety of recall strategies, most based on the simple premise that the last n recent user inputs are a reasonable working set of candidates for reselection. But is this premise correct? Might other strategies work better? Indeed, is the dialog sufficiently repetitive to warrant some type of activity reuse facility in the first place? As existing reuse facilities were designed by intuition rather than from empirical knowledge of user interactions, it is difficult to judge how effective they really are or what scope there is for improvement.

The next four chapters of this book explore the possibility of people reusing (as opposed to reentering) their previous activities. This chapter surveys and provides examples of interactive reuse facilities that allow users to recall, modify, and resubmit their previous entries to computers. Although the idea is simple – anything used before can be used again – it is effective only when recalling old activities is less work for the user (cognitively and physically) than submitting new ones. As we shall see in this chapter, the main differences between reuse facilities arise from their ability to offer a reasonable set of candidates for reselection, and from the user interface available to manipulate these candidates.

For example, consider a user who has submitted n activities to the system (say $n > 100$) and whose next activity is identical to a previous one. An optimal reuse facility would be an oracle that correctly predicted when an old action could be reused and submitted it to the system in the user's stead. In contrast, a non-predictive system that merely presents the user with all previous n submissions would be less effective, for the user's overhead now includes scanning (or remembering) the complete interaction history and selecting the desired action. Real systems are situated between these extremes. A small set of reasonable predictions p is offered to the user ($p << n$), sometimes ranked by probability. The intention is to make the act of selecting a prediction less work than entering it anew; the metric for "work" is, of course, ill defined.

Reuse facilities have loose analogies in non-computer contexts. A cook can explicitly mark preferred recipes in a cookbook by using bookmarks (n = total recipes used, p = total bookmarks). "Adaptive" marking takes place when the book naturally opens to highly used locations through wear of the binding and food-encrusted pages. Or consider the audiophile who places records just listened to at the top of the pile. Assuming that certain records are favored over others, popular records tend to remain near the top of the stack and unpopular ones near the bottom. A carpenter's workbench has an implicit reuse facility – the work surface is large enough to leave recently used tools on hand.

Three kinds of reuse facilities are distinguished in the following sections. The first covers *history mechanisms* that let users manipulate a temporally ordered list of their interactions. The second, *adaptive systems*, uses dynamic models of previous inputs to predict subsequent ones, which are then made available to the user. Finally, *programming by example* is concerned with reuse and generalization of long input sequences.

The three subsequent chapters will assume an experimental approach to reuse. Analyses of data and discussions are focused toward seeing how people repeat their activities on UNIX and other systems, and the results are distilled into design principles for empirically based reuse facilities.

4.1 History mechanisms

History mechanisms assume that the last few user submissions are good candidates to make available for reuse. This notion of "temporal recency" is cognitively attractive because users generally remember what they have just entered and can predict the offerings the system will make available to them. Little time is wasted searching in vain for missing items.

History mechanisms are by far the most common reuse facility available, and are implemented across diverse systems in a variety of flavors. Four fundamentally different interaction styles are described in this section: glass teletypes; graphical selection; editing transcripts; and navigational traces. The first three pertain to command line interfaces, whereas the last applies to systems in which users traverse some information structure.

4.1.1   History in glass teletypes

Traditional command line dialogs were created for the teletype; as a result many of today's VDUs are still a fixed viewport into a virtual roll of paper. Two functionally rich history systems designed for these physically limited "glass teletypes" are the UNIX *csh* and the INTERLISP–D *programmer's assistant*. Both systems have users retrieve old commands by "history directives," which are themselves commands interpreted in a special way.

UNIX *csh* maintains an invisible record of user inputs, where every string entered on the command line is recorded in a numbered event list (Joy, 1980). Special syntactic constructs allow previous events to be partially or completely recalled, either by position on the list (relative or absolute) or by pattern matching. The recalled events can be viewed, edited, and reexecuted. Even though the set of predictions is in principle unbounded, in practice it is small for users will forget all but the last few items they have entered. Although users may request a snapshot of the event list, they usually choose not to because of the extra work and time involved.

Figure 4.1 illustrates an event list (top box) and a few possibilities of *csh* history in use on the next event (bottom box). Inputs in the bottom left column are translated by *csh* to the actions shown in the middle, and the right column describes the semantics of the history directives. As the examples illustrate, the syntax is quite arcane, and deters use of the more powerful features (see Chapter 6; also Lee and Lochovsky, 1990). Because the event list is generally invisible – snapshots of its current state are displayed only by special request – it is difficult for the *csh* user to refer to any but the last few events.

Another functionally powerful history mechanism is the *programmer's assistant*, designed for the INTERLISP–D programming environment (Teitelman and Masinter, 1981; Xerox, 1985). Although INTERLISP–D is window-based, the top-level "Interlisp-D Executive" occupies a plain scrolling window (a glass teletype) where the user types lisp expressions (Figure 4.2). The user can also select and process historical events by typing special command directives into this window, which are interpreted by the *programmer's assistant*. For example, the request *USE cons FOR setq IN –1* will replace the string "setq" by "cons" in the previous command. The *programmer's assistant* history mechanism is functionally richer than UNIX *csh*. Through its history mechanism, users can retrieve and manipulate several events at a time, specify iteration and conditionals, edit items, undo effects of previous entries, and so on. Figure 4.2 shows a sample dialog in the window labeled "Interlisp-D Executive," where events 85 and 87 make use of the *programmer's assistant*. As with *csh*, the system maintains a true time-ordered event list – every entry is shown, even duplicates and erroneous statements.

Example Event List	
9	mail ian
10	emacs fig1 fig2 fig3
11	cat fig1
12	diff fig*

Examples and Results of History Uses		
User Input	**Action**	**Description**
!!	diff fig*	Redo the last event
!11	cat fig1	Redo event 11
!-2	cat fig1	Redo the second event from last
!mai	mail ian	Redo last event with prefix "mail"
!?ian?	mail ian	Redo last event containing the string "ian"
!! fig3	diff fig* fig3	Append "fig3" to the last event and redo
∧diff∧page	page fig*	Substitute "page" for "diff" in the last command
!!:p	diff fig*	Print without executing the last event
page !10:1-2	page fig1 fig2	Include the 1st and 2nd arguments of event 10 and redo

Figure 4.1. Examples of the UNIX *csh* history mechanism in use.

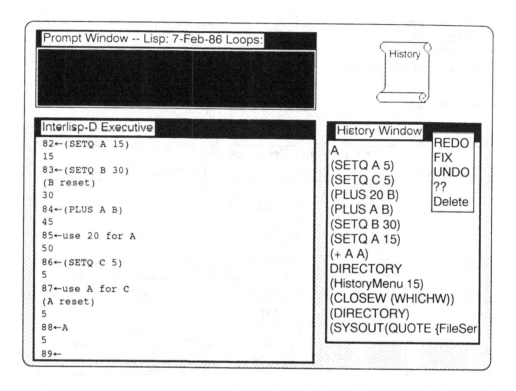

Figure 4.2. A portion of the INTERLISP–D environment, showing HISTMENU in use.

4.1.2   History through graphical selection

Present-day terminals allow text to be placed anywhere on the screen, and high-resolution bitmapped workstations with a pointing device (usually a mouse) are common. Interaction styles have progressed accordingly, from text-oriented menus and forms to mouse-oriented graphical systems running within windows (Witten and Greenberg, 1985). History mechanisms have been extended to present a (possibly transient) menu of previous events, where items are selected and manipulated with the pointing device. In contrast to previous history mechanisms that relied heavily on a user's memory of submissions and their relative ordering, predictions are now offered by presenting them explicitly on the screen. Because selection is usually just a matter of pointing to the desired item, the syntactic knowledge required by the user is kept to a minimum.

One example is HISTMENU, which provides a limited yet simple way of accessing and modifying the INTERLISP–D *programmer's assistant* history list (Bobrow, 1986). Figure 4.2 illustrates its use. Commands entered to the "INTERLISP–D

Executive" window are recorded on the history list, part of which is displayed in the "History Window" (by default, the last fifty items are shown; we show only thirteen in the figure). Although the internal list is updated on every command, the window is redrawn only when the user explicitly requests it. When pointed at with a mouse, items (which may not fit completely in the narrow history window) are printed in the "Prompt Window" (top of figure). Any entry can be reexecuted by selecting it. Moreover, a pop-up menu allows limited further action: items can be "fixed" (i.e., edited), undone, printed in full including additional detail (the "??"), or deleted. The history window also has a shrunken form, as shown by the icon in the figure.

MINIT is another graphical package that combines command processing and the history list into a single WINDOW MANAGEMENT WINDOW (Barnes and Bovey, 1986). It differs from other systems in that only through this window can the user send commands to the other windows. The WINDOW MANAGEMENT WINDOW is divided into three regions (Figure 4.3). The bottom region is an editable typing line in which commands are typed. Once entered, they are automatically added to the second region that contains a scrollable history list. As with HISTMENU, the user may select items using a pointing device and control further action with a pop-up menu – options are available to execute the item in various windows and to insert the item into the typing line for further editing. The final region at the top of Figure 4.3 contains a history management menu. Options are available to

- scroll the history list, clear it, or save it for future use;
- textually search for specific items;
- delete specific items;
- insert text in the typing line without executing it.

Two more mechanisms complete MINIT's history management capabilities. First, the user can customize the system to prevent short commands that are easily retyped from being added to the list. Second, history is viewable in either alphabetical or execution order. Duplicate lines are eliminated in both methods. In execution order, the user controls whether the original of a repeated command entry remains in its original position or is moved to the end of the history list.

It is less easy to provide a history facility for a graphical interface such as a painting or drawing program, and we are aware of only one system that comes close to offering such capabilities. CHIMERA adopts the metaphor of a "comic strip," a graphical record of the user's past activities that consists of a sequence of panels, each of which illustrates an important moment in a story (Kurlander and Feiner, 1990). Instead of showing miniatures, panels record just the objects being manipulated and the actions performed on them without unnecessary detail. This graphical history provides more power than just reuse, and it is far closer

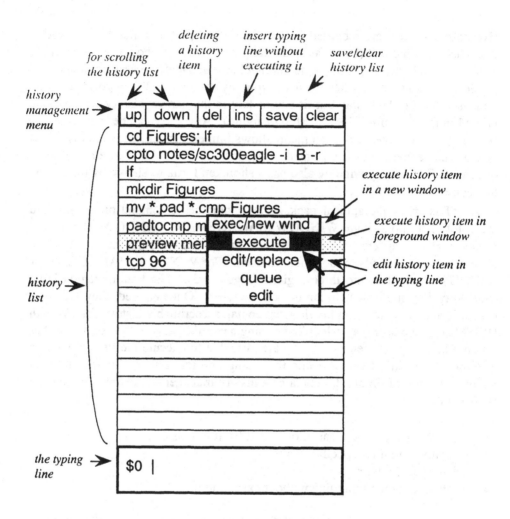

Figure 4.3. MINIT's WINDOW MANAGEMENT WINDOW, redrawn from Barnes and Bovey (1986).

in spirit to a full undo, skip, and redo facility (Vitter, 1984). The user can then: expand a particular panel as necessary; delete, modify, undo, and redo the actions it expresses; and even add new actions into the sequence.

4.1.3 History by editing transcripts

Some systems do not have a command history mechanism per se, but provide similar capabilities through editing a transcript of the dialog. Instead of having the sequential text dialog scroll off the screen (as with a glass teletype), it can be maintained as a scrollable transcript. When text appearing previously can be selected and used as input to the system, the transcript becomes a rudimentary history mechanism.[1]

Copy and paste capabilities are available in most modern-day window-based environments, where any text can be copied and pasted anywhere else. A typical example is VERSATERM, a terminal emulator for the Apple Macintosh that maintains the transcript in a scrollable window (Figure 4.4).[2]   As shown in the figure, text appearing within the transcript can be selected, then copied and pasted by choosing the pull-down menu option. This will insert the text into the command input area after the text cursor at the window's bottom, where it may be edited as needed. Explicit history lists are not maintained except as part of the scrollable dialog transcript. Although there are some slight interface differences, many other popular window-based terminal emulators allow one to select a text region anywhere on the display and paste it to the command input area, for example, *xterm* within the standard X window system (Quercia and O'Reilly, 1990), *pads* within APOLLOs DOMAIN window system (Apollo, 1986), and the *command tool* within the OPEN LOOK DESKSET environment (Sun, 1990). Although *any* text in a transcript is potentially executable in all these systems, the tradeoff is that mixing previous input commands with output makes useful candidates more difficult to find.

Another example is *emacs*, an editing environment that provides multiple views of buffers through tiled windows (Stallman, 1981). Although buffers typically allow users to view and edit files, it is also possible to run interactive processes (or programs) within them. In most implementations of *emacs*, it is a simple matter to call up a window running UNIX *csh* (e.g., Stallman, 1987; Unipress, 1986). All capabilities of *emacs* are then available – commands may be edited, sessions scrolled, pieces of text picked up from any buffer and used as input, and so on.

A further variant of transcript editing is the *zmacs* editor running within the

---

[1]The ability to scroll over a session's transcript and select text for reexecution goes by a variety of names: spatial browsing (Kurlander and Feiner, 1990), history through command typescripts by direct manipulation (Lee, 1990), and history by editing transcripts (this chapter).

[2]VERSATERM 4.0 software produced by Abelbeck Software.

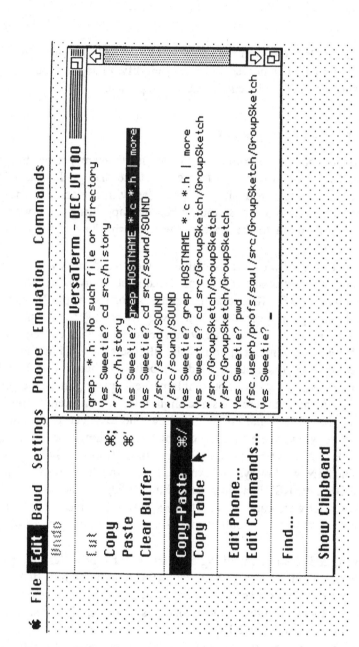

Figure 4.4. The VERSATERM terminal emulator for the Apple Macintosh. A user redoes a UNIX submission by copying and pasting an old command line from the transcript to the command input area.

SYMBOLICS GENERA lisp environment. This editor contains features of all history systems discussed so far (Symbolics, 1985). Within the top-level lisp listener, *zmacs* extends the functionality of *emacs*. Although used here primarily for entering and editing command lines, previous inputs appearing within the transcript become mouse-sensitive. A box appears around them as the mouse passes over them, and pressing one mouse button copies the old command line into the input area and makes it available for editing. Other button combinations immediately reexecute previous commands, copy arbitrary command words, show context-sensitive documentation, and so on. Alternatively, part or all of the mouse-sensitive event list can be displayed within the lisp listener window. Keyboard-based retrieval is also available within *zmacs*. Using the standard editing commands within the one-line input area, a user can search, cycle through, and recall previous events, similar to the command line capabilities of the VMS operating system (DEC, 1985), the UNIX *tcsh* (Greer, Ellis, Placeway, and Zachariassen, 1991), and GNU *emacs* (Stallman, 1987).

4.1.4 History by navigational traces

History has been applied to information retrieval and to systems where items must be retrieved by some navigational process. These include traversing menu hierarchies, searching through file directories, navigating hypertext, and so on. Here, history can record both the route paths taken through the information structure and the actual information finally selected, and then allow users to travel quickly through previously traveled paths and choose old items.

In many systems, users tend to retrieve items of information that have been accessed previously (Greenberg and Witten, 1985a). The assumption that previously read documents are referred to many times has been supported by a study of *man*, the UNIX on-line manual (see Section 5.3.1; also Greenberg, 1984). Each user frequently retrieved the same small set of pages from the large set that was available, where sets differed substantially between users. By keeping a history list of the documentation retrieved or nodes selected, users can avoid renavigating the path to a previously viewed topic. Because items on the list can be viewed as placeholders in a large document, they are sometimes known as "bookmarks."

The Macintosh HYPERCARD is a simple hypertext facility that allows authoring and browsing of stacks of information comprised of cards. Navigating cross-links between stacks and cards is usually accomplished by simple button or menu selections. *Recent* is a history facility within HYPERCARD that maintains a pictoral list of up to the last forty-two unique cards visited (Figure 4.5). Each picture is a miniature view of the card, placed on the list in order of first appearance.[3]

---

[3]Figure 4.5 is a fairly accurate representation of the screen. Because these miniature pictures are of poor quality, the value of the current *recent* implementation is questionable. However, this problem could be overcome

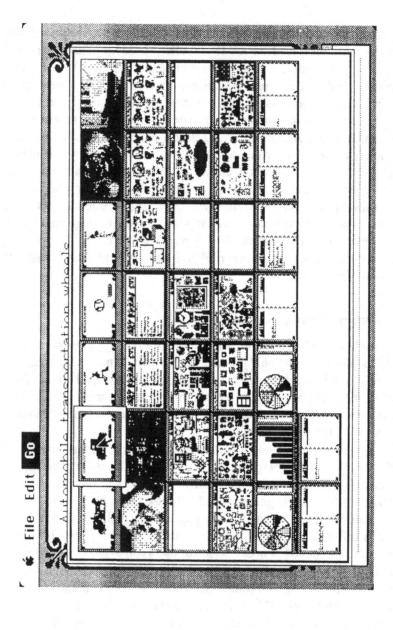

Figure 4.5. The HYPERCARD *recent* screen.

The last card visited is distinguished by a larger border, as illustrated by the second miniature in the first row of the figure. A pull-down menu option pops up the *recent* display, and old cards are revisited by selecting their miniatures from the list (Goodman, 1987). When more than forty-two unique items have been selected, the first row of seven items is cleared and made available for new ones (even though a card in the first row may have recently been selected).

Feiner, Nagy, and van Dam (1982) push the notion of miniatures even further in their experimental hypertext system. Hypertext nodes contain images that are displayed on a document page; the page comprises the image plus controls for moving between pages. One control is the "back page" button, a miniaturized image of the last page visited with the word "back" overlaid on top of it. Selecting this control will replace the current page with the last one visited. More complex is the special "timeline" page, a time-stamped event list of the pages visited. What makes it interesting is that miniatures are presented in a scrollable two-dimensional grid. The horizontal axis represents chronological order, and the vertical axis represents the chapters in the document. Miniatures of the visited pages are positioned on the grid by their parent chapter and chronological order of selection. As with the "back page" button, selecting a miniature will transport the reader back to that page.

The SYMBOLICS environment includes a very large on-line manual viewable with the DOCUMENT EXAMINER – a window-based hypertext system (Symbolics, 1985). The main window is divided into functionally different panes: a documentation display area, a menu of topics, a bookmarks area, and a command line. The bookmarks area displays a history list of previously viewed topics, where each title is a bookmark. Further bookmarks may be explicitly added by the user (these are visually distinguished from historical bookmarks). Selecting a bookmark displays either full documentation or a brief summary of the topic in the documentation area. A similar bookmark strategy has been proposed previously for videotext systems (Engel, Andriessen, and Schmitz, 1983).

These reuse techniques are not limited to document navigation. Navigation occurs in many human–computer interfaces, from hierarchical menu and folder systems, to structured browsers for programming systems. Many modern window environments now supply graphical file browsers to let users visually navigate through their (usually hierarchical) file stores. Some include history facilities. FILE MANAGER, the file browser provided in the OPEN LOOK DESKSET environment, keeps a history list of all directories through which the user has navigated (Sun, 1990). Figure 4.6 illustrates its use. The list can be popped up as a menu by selecting the "Home" button, and selecting any of the directory paths presented will immediately bring the user there. As with *recent*, items are presented in their order of first appearance. A more elaborate scheme is available on the Apple

---

by higher-resolution miniatures or perhaps by including a "magnifying glass."

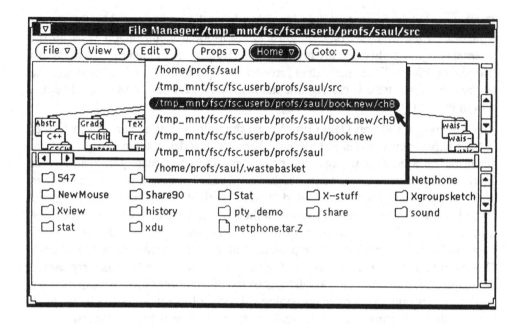

Figure 4.6. A sample FILE MANAGER window, showing a history list of the last few files visited.

Macintosh. Within an application, a file is usually opened through an "open dialog box," a simple mechanism that lets users navigate up and down a folder hierarchy, with files shown as a scrollable and selectable list (left side of Figure 4.7). Whereas the basic system has minimal support for history – the previously opened folder is presented by default to the user – a third party system called BOOMERANG adds full history support onto the open dialog box.[4] The menu on the right side of Figure 4.7 shows a person using BOOMERANG's top-level menu to access a history-ordered list of previously opened files (files that cannot be opened by the current application are grayed out and are not selectable). Similar functionality is also available for folders and for disks.

4.2 Adaptive systems

History mechanisms model the user's previous inputs by recording them in a time-ordered list. Adaptive systems build more elaborate statistical dynamic models and

---

[4]BOOMERANG 2.0 developed by Zeta Soft (H. Yamamoto) and distributed by Now Software, 2425B ChanningWy, Suite 492, Berkeley, California.

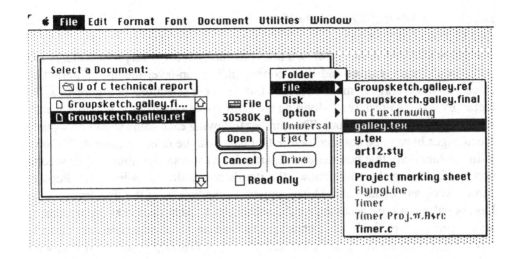

Figure 4.7. The Apple Macintosh "open dialog" box, showing the BOOMERANG history menu.

use them to predict subsequent inputs, which are presented to the user for selection or approval. In this section we will describe two types of adaptive systems, one for accelerating selection in a hierarchical menu system and the other for the entry of free text. Both employ predominantly frequency-based, rather than recency-based, models.

4.2.1 Adaptive menu hierarchies

It is possible to devise interactive menu-based interfaces that dynamically reconfigure a menu hierarchy so that high-frequency items are treated preferentially, at the expense of low-frequency items. ADAPTIVE MENUS provide an attractive way of reducing the average number of choices that a user must make to select an item without adding further paraphernalia to the interface (Witten, Cleary, and Greenberg, 1984; Greenberg, 1984). Consider a telephone directory where the access frequencies of names combined with their recency of selection define a probability distribution on the set of entries, which reflects the "popularity" of the names selected (Greenberg and Witten, 1985a). Instead of selecting regions at each stage to cover approximately equal ranges of names, it is possible to divide the probability distribution into approximately equal portions. During use, the act of selection will alter the distribution and thereby increase the probability of the names selected. Thus the user will be directed more quickly to entries that have already been selected – especially if they have been selected often and recently – than to those that have not.

Figures 4.8a and 4.8b depict two menu hierarchies for a very small dictionary with twenty name entries and their corresponding top-level menus. Figure 4.8c calculates the average number of menus traversed per selection. In Figure 4.8a, the hierarchy was obtained by subdividing the name space as equally as possible at each stage, with a menu size of four. The number following each name shows how many menu pages have to be scanned before that name can be found. Figure 4.8b shows a similar hierarchy that now reflects a particular frequency distribution (the second number following the name shows the item's probability of selection). Popular names, such as Graham and Zlotky, appear immediately on the first-level menu. Less popular ones are accessed on the second-level menu, whereas the remainder are relegated to the third level. For this particular case, the average number of menus traversed by probability subdivision is less with probability subdivision than with uniform subdivision, although this improvement is not as much as is theoretically possible (Figure 4.8c). As probabilities also decay over time, once-popular (or erroneously chosen) names eventually drop to a low value. A decay factor also builds in a way of balancing frequency and recency. Whereas low decay will see frequently chosen items migrate up the tree, a high decay rate gives more room to recently chosen items.

Given a frequency distribution, it is not easy to construct a menu hierarchy that minimizes the average number of selections required to find a name. Exhaustive search over all menu trees is infeasible for all but the smallest problems. However, simple splitting algorithms achieve good (but not optimal) performance in practice (Witten, Cleary, and Greenberg, 1984).

With ADAPTIVE MENUS, previous actions are almost always easier to resubmit. Also, because no extra detail is added to the interface presentation, screen usage is minimized. However, users must now scan the menus for their entries all the time, even for those accessed frequently. Because paths change dynamically, memory cannot be used to bypass the search process. Experimental evidence suggests that this is not a problem in practice. As long as the database of entries is large, the benefits will usually outweigh the deficiencies (Greenberg and Witten, 1985a). It is also possible to have the system monitor the average depth of the menu selection process over time. If for some reason the average depth increased beyond what would be normally expected, a static menu system could be substituted for the adaptive one

4.2.2 *Reuse through text prediction*

History facilities assume that the last submissions entered are likely candidates for reexecution. They are the ones visible on the screen in graphical and editing systems, the ones most easily remembered by the user in glass teletypes, and the

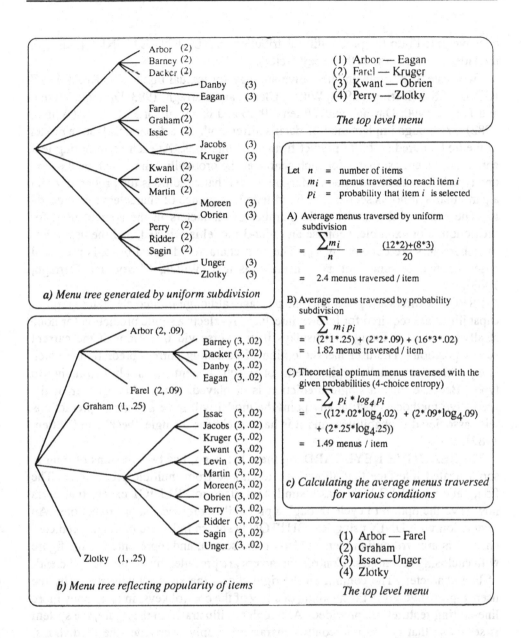

a) Menu tree generated by uniform subdivision

(1) Arbor — Eagan
(2) Farel — Kruger
(3) Kwant — Obrien
(4) Perry — Zlotky

The top level menu

Let n = number of items
      m_i = menus traversed to reach item i
      p_i = probability that item i is selected

A) Average menus traversed by uniform subdivision

$$= \frac{\sum m_i}{n} = \frac{(12*2)+(8*3)}{20}$$

$$= 2.4 \text{ menus traversed / item}$$

B) Average menus traversed by probability subdivision

$$= \sum m_i p_i$$
$$= (2*1*.25) + (2*2*.09) + (16*3*.02)$$
$$= 1.82 \text{ menus traversed / item}$$

C) Theoretical optimum menus traversed with the given probabilities (4-choice entropy)

$$= -\sum p_i * \log_4 p_i$$
$$= -((12*.02*\log_4.02) + (2*.09*\log_4.09)$$
$$+ (2*.25*\log_4.25))$$
$$= 1.49 \text{ menus / item}$$

c) Calculating the average menus traversed for various conditions

b) Menu tree reflecting popularity of items

(1) Arbor — Farel
(2) Graham
(3) Issac—Unger
(4) Zlotky

The top level menu

Figure 4.8. **Menu trees generated by uniform and probability subdivision.**

ones weighted into the probability distribution in ADAPTIVE MENUS (although the latter is a function of the decay factor).

Two systems provide an alternative strategy for textual input – the REACTIVE KEYBOARD (Darragh, 1988; Witten, Cleary, and Darragh, 1983; Darragh, Witten, and James, 1990; Darragh and Witten, 1992) and its precursor PREDICT (Witten, 1982).[5] Although implementation details differ, both use a dynamic adaptive model of the text entered so far to predict further submissions. At each point during text entry, the system estimates for each character the probability that it will be the next one typed. This is based upon a Markov model that conditions the probability that a particular symbol is seen on the fixed-length sequence of characters that precede it. The order of the model is the number of characters in the context used for prediction. For example, suppose an order-3 model is selected, and the user's last two characters are denoted by xy. The next character, denoted by ϕ, is predicted based upon occurrences of $xy\phi$ in previous text (Witten, Cleary, and Darragh, 1983).

PREDICT filters any glass-teletype package, although limited character graphics capabilities are required for its own interface. It selects a single prediction (or none at all) as the most likely and displays it in reverse video in front of the current cursor position. The user has the option of accepting correct predictions, which is equivalent to actually typing them, or rejecting them by simply continuing to type. Because only a single prediction is displayed, much of the power of the predictive method is lost; at any point the model will have a range of predictions with associated probabilities, and it is hard to choose a single "best" one (Witten, 1982).

The REACTIVE KEYBOARD, on the other hand, has two versions of a more sophisticated interface that allows one to choose from multiple predictions. The first, called RK-BUTTON, has a similar interface to PREDICT except that users now have the option to cycle through a probability-ordered list of predictions. An interaction with UNIX using RK-BUTTON is shown in Figure 4.9. The predicted characters are written in reverse video on the screen, and represented in the figure with enclosing rectangles. Control characters are preceded by ∧, and ∧J is the end-of-line character. The column on the right shows the keys actually struck by the user. Figure 4.9b gives the meaning of a few of the control keys; in fact, many more line-editing features are provided. Although not illustrated in the figure, the system is set up so that typing non-control characters simply overwrites the predictions; thus one may use the keyboard in the ordinary way without even looking at the screen.

The second version of the REACTIVE KEYBOARD, called RK-POINTER, displays a menu containing the best p predictions, which changes dynamically

[5]These systems, their use, and their algorithms are completely described in another book in the Cambridge Series on Human–Computer Interaction (Darragh and Witten, 1992).

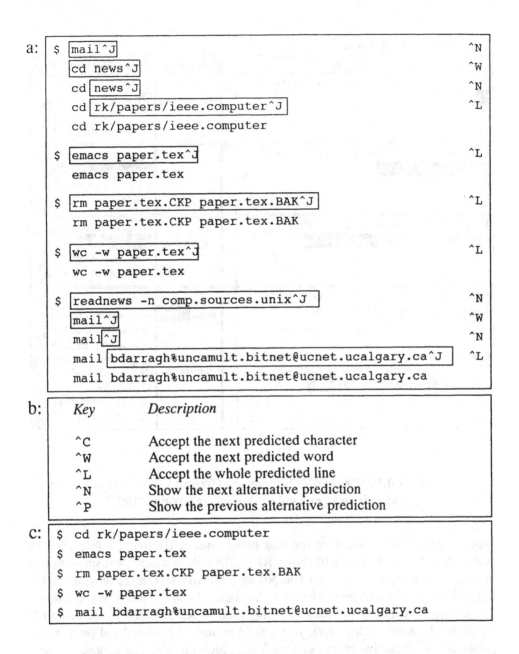

Figure 4.9. Using RK-BUTTON, the UNIX version of the REACTIVE KEYBOARD: (a) a dialog with UNIX; (b) some commands; and (c) screen contents at end of the dialog.

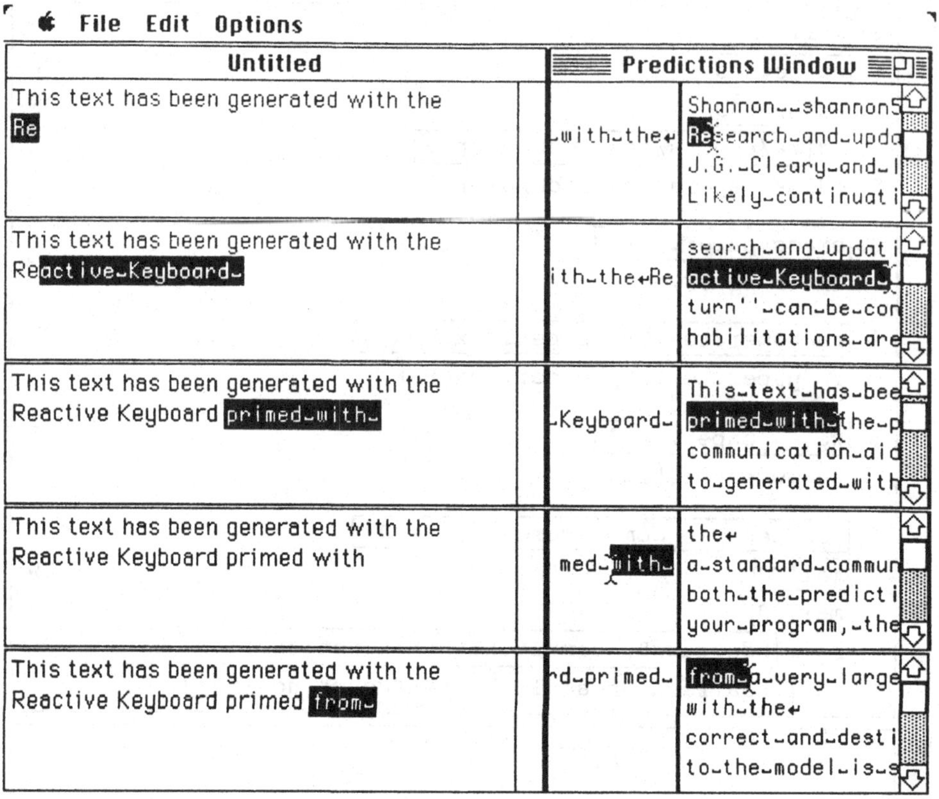

Untitled		Predictions Window ▤□▤
This text has been generated with the `Re`	⌐with⌐the⤶ `Re`search⌐and⌐upda⌐	Shannon⌐⌐shannonS J.G.⌐Cleary⌐and⌐I Likely⌐continuati
This text has been generated with the Re`active⌐Keyboard⌐`	ith⌐the⤶Re `active⌐Keyboard⌐`	search⌐and⌐updati turn''⌐can⌐be⌐con habilitations⌐are
This text has been generated with the Reactive Keyboard `primed⌐with⌐`	⌐Keyboard⌐ `primed⌐with⌐`the⌐p	This⌐text⌐has⌐bee communication⌐aic to⌐generated⌐with
This text has been generated with the Reactive Keyboard primed with	med⌐`with⌐`	the⤶ a⌐standard⌐commun both⌐the⌐predicti your⌐program,⌐the
This text has been generated with the Reactive Keyboard primed `from⌐`	⌐d⌐primed⌐	`from⌐`a⌐very⌐large with⌐the⤶ correct⌐and⌐desti to⌐the⌐model⌐is⌐s

Figure 4.10. RK-POINTER menu and feedback showing five interaction sequences; from Figure 4.4 in Darragh and Witten (1992).

with the immediate context of the text being entered (Darragh, 1988; Darragh and Witten, 1992). Figure 4.10 shows RK-POINTER in action by displaying five interaction sequences of the user composing some free text in the window on the left, with a window of predictions on the right. In the "Predictions Window," the left region contains the context string upon which predictions are made (its length is adjustable by the user). In the right region are rank-ordered predictions, presented as alternative pieces of text from which the user can choose the next characters. Interaction is through a pointing device, such as a mouse. Selection is two-dimensional, in that the user can point anywhere within a prediction to accept only the previous characters (the selected characters are shown in reverse video in Figure 4.10). Less likely predictions are available through page-turning.

Text prediction based upon adaptive modeling appears promising. Keystroke reductions of 50% and 90% have been achieved with PREDICT and the REACTIVE

KEYBOARD, respectively. However, these figures depend heavily on the type of text entered and how the system has been primed. Considerable variation is likely in practice. Theoretical benefits are also tempered by practical considerations. If the cognitive and mechanical task of reviewing and (perhaps) accepting predictions takes more time than simple text reentry, then keystroke reduction becomes a misleading measure of the system's overall performance. Furthermore, as users themselves may not be able to predict the system's offerings, they must scan the list to see if a desired item is present. It is certain that a skilled typist will be capable of entering free text faster than someone using the REACTIVE KEYBOARD, for the time needed to review the predictions offered after every keystroke is far longer than the time required just to type it in. However, these are powerful systems for physically disabled people (see also Greenberg, Darragh, Maulsby, and Witten, 1993). As Darragh notes:

> Of all potential users, those with severe physical limitations and communication disabilities stand to gain the most from the REACTIVE KEYBOARD. Certain individuals within this group will find the REACTIVE KEYBOARD a valuable time and energy saving enhancement (or replacement) for their standard communication aid when writing or accessing computer systems.
> — Darragh, 1988, p. 133

Systems that predict character sequences are appealing because they deal with any free text. They are not limited, as history mechanisms are, to repeating lines or other forms of incremental command submission. Yet this generality is also their weakness when used as a front end to the command-based systems. There is no guarantee that predictions will form valid command lines, because the underlying Markov model has no knowledge about (say) UNIX. There is nothing to stop predictions from being either syntactically malformed or nonsensical.

On the other hand, predictive systems have, for at least one person, proven effective for *csh* interaction. Darragh, who is partially paralyzed, mentioned that RK-BUTTON was (and is) indispensable for his day-to-day computer use. It provided assistance on over thirty thousand command lines over a two-year period, and averaged ten character predictions per line (Darragh, 1988, p. 136). He has received similar comments on its helpfulness from other disabled users. He also notes an interesting side effect – long descriptive file names are now used instead of short ones.

4.3 Reuse through programming by example

The schemes discussed so far attempt to facilitate the reuse of individual items of activity, such as commands, command lines, menu selections, or characters predicted in context. This is sufficient if incremental activities have a one-to-one correspondence with tasks the user may wish to repeat later. Often, however, tasks are accomplished by sequences of several primitive activities.

Closure is defined as the user's subjective sense of reaching a goal, of completion, or of understanding (Thimbleby, 1980). Previous sections have assumed that closure is associated with each individual user action (the entry of a command or command line, the selection of a document, and so on). If the task to be redone involves a sequence of such activities, even though they are all independently available through a reuse facility, the user would have to decompose mentally his task into its primitives and choose each of them from the event list. For example, viewing a specific file can comprise two activities: navigating to the correct directory, and printing the desired file to the screen. In some cases, it will be easier for the user to think about and recall these items as a single chunk rather than as two separate activities.

When tasks are a sequence of activities, they constitute a procedure that can be specified by the user giving one or more examples of the instance of the sequence. The goal of *programming by example* is to allow sequences and more complex constructs to be communicated concretely, without the user resorting to abstract specifications of control and data structure (e.g., in a programming language) (Witten, MacDonald, and Greenberg, 1987; Myers, 1986)

The simplest programming by example procedure is a verbatim playback of a sequence. The user performs an example of the required procedure and the system remembers it for later repetition. For example, the use of "start-remembering," "stop-remembering," and "do-it" commands enables a text editor to store and play back macros of editing sequences (Gosling, 1981; Stallman, 1987; Unipress, 1986). Except for these special commands, the macro sequence is completely specified by normal editing operations. With a little more effort, such sequences can be named, filed for later use, and even edited (if presented in a human-readable form). A practical difficulty with having a special mode – remembering mode – for recording a sequence is that frequently one has already started the sequence before deciding to record it, and so must retrace one's steps and begin again.

The ability to generalize these simple macros could extend their power enormously. Some programming by example strategies allow inclusion of standard programming concepts – variables, conditionals, iteration, and so on – either by inference from a number of sample sequences, or through explicit elaboration of an example by the user. To illustrate the latter, an experimental system called SMALLSTAR has been constructed for the Xerox Star office workstation that operates according to the direct manipulation paradigm (Halbert, 1981; Halbert, 1984) In the first version of SMALLSTAR, a pop-up menu allowed one to indicate explicitly the generalization required. For example, icons selected at specification time are disambiguated by name, by position, or by asking for a similar object. But because people found it hard to elaborate programming constructs when tracing through an example, a later version had users employ an editor to specify constructs after macro composition (Halbert, 1984).

Reminiscent of the editing capabilities of SMALLSTAR is QUICKEYS, a commercial macro facility for the Apple Macintosh.[6] Through a pull-down menu (left side of Figure 4.11), the user can start, stop, and pause recording sequences, choose selected macros for playback (there are two shown at the bottom of the menu), and look at a reference card containing all the macros that have been recorded previously. Once a macro has been defined, it may be edited. The right side of Figure 4.11 shows a user editing a macro sequence she has named "Open Database" (background window). A mouse "click" primitive, which was used to open a window, has been chosen (middle window), and the user now has the option of having QUICKEYS find the window by its name on playback, rather than by its position on the window stack. The problem is that editing takes much detective work to find the correct primitive, for operations are recorded and presented at a very low syntactic level (such as a mouse click) instead of its semantic meaning (such as opening a particular window). Only after navigating through several presentation screens will the user discover what the mouse click really does.

Other research on programming by example has concentrated on inferring control constructs from traces of execution given by the user (Witten, MacDonald, and Greenberg, 1987), and some systems use domain knowledge, teaching metaphors, and highly interactive interfaces to maximize the speed of transfer of procedures (e.g., Maulsby and Witten, 1989; Maulsby, Witten, and Kittlitz, 1989; Maulsby, Witten, Kittlitz, and Franceschin, 1991). However, there has been little research on ways of naming, filing, and accessing procedures taught by example, and particularly on knowledge and history-based methods of splitting up a stream of activities into user-oriented "tasks." This limits the practical use of programming by example in reuse systems.

The appeal of programming by example is the belief that a user's activity follows a preconceived plan that can be encapsulated as a procedure. Intentions are realized as plans-for-actions that directly guide behavior, and plans are actually prescriptions or instructions for actions. These plans reduce to a detailed set of instructions (which may also be subplans) that actually serve as the program that controls the action. Suchman (1987) disputes this notion by claiming that plans are derived from situated action – the necessarily ad hoc responses to the contingencies of particular situations. Initial plans must be inherently vague if they are to accommodate the unforeseeable contingencies of actual situations of action. It is only the post hoc analysis of situated action that makes it appear as if a rational plan were followed. Assuming that user activity on computers does arise from situated action, then a programming by example system would not suffice by itself as a complete user support tool, for it would not respond well to the changing circumstances of situations. When previous actions are collected as fixed goal-related scripts of

---

[6]QUICKEYS is produced by CE Software Incorporated.

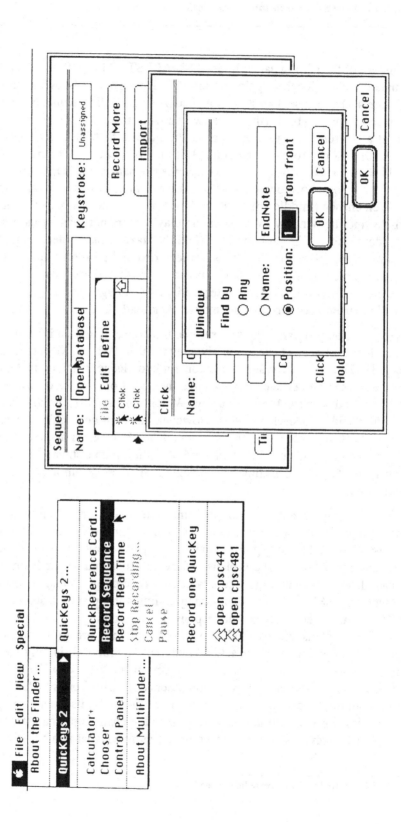

Figure 4.11. The QUICKEYS menu and several sequence-editing windows.

events, flexibility is lost. It should be augmented by a reuse facility that collects the actual responses to given situations, allowing one to select, possibly modify, and redo the individual activities.

4.4 Concluding remarks

A reuse facility arranges for submissions entered to the application to be collected and presented so that they are available for reuse. Three classes of reuse facility were distinguished in this chapter: history mechanisms, adaptive systems, and programming by example. A large number of ad hoc implemented designs were surveyed within this framework, illustrating the diversity of techniques available. Their appeal is the assistance they offer in any dialog that exhibits recurrence. Because no semantic knowledge of the domain is usually needed, it is quite a general approach. However, particular methods appear less than promising because the cognitive and mechanical effort required to reuse most old submissions is obviously greater than entering them anew.

The taxonomy of reuse facilities presented in this chapter is oriented toward a survey of designs, and is certainly not the only structure possible. The mechanism underlying reuse facilities – monitoring the user's interaction and maintaining an internal model of it – has potential for supplying more extensive user support. For example, Lee (1988, 1990) gives the following eight ways that people could make use of a history model.[7]

1. *History for reuse* allows a person to reuse an old item.
2. *Relating input and output* is a more specialized form of reuse, for it further describes and disambiguates the objects and actions of reference in the context of the dialog.
3. *History through navigation* allows users to reflect on where they have been and where they are now, and use it to guide their progress.
4. *History through user recovery* includes undo capabilities.
5. *History for functional grouping* lets users group a set of history items into a functional unit.
6. *Recording and playback* covers verbatim replay of action sequences.
7. *History for consultations and reminders* allows the user to consult past actions and provides the user with reminders.
8. *History for prediction* helps anticipate and predict what the next user command would be.

A key deficiency in this general area is the absence of empirical evidence justi-

---

[7]Lee's distinctions cite and incorporate the ones made in this chapter.

fying designs for reuse facilities, either a priori through knowledge of how people repeat activities, or post hoc by evaluating their actual use. Nor are there any guidelines for how intuitive and empirical knowledge gleaned from one application might generalize to others. The next three chapters address these deficiencies.

5

Recurrent systems

Schemes for activity reuse are based upon the assumption that the human–computer dialog has many recurring activities. Yet there is almost no empirical evidence confirming the existence of these recurrences or suggestions of how observed patterns of recurrences in one dialog would generalize to other dialogs. The next few chapters address this dearth. They provide empirical evidence that people not only repeat their activities, but that they do so in quite regular ways.[1] This chapter starts with the general notion of *recurrent systems*, where most users predominantly repeat their previous activities. Such systems suggest potential for activity reuse because there is opportunity to give preferential treatment to the large number of repeated actions. A few suspected recurrent systems from both non-computer and computer domains are examined in this context to help pinpoint salient features. Particular attention is paid to repetition of activities in telephone use, information retrieval in technical manuals, and command lines in UNIX. The following chapters further examine UNIX as a recurrent system, and then generalize the results obtained into a set of design properties.

5.1 A definition of recurrent systems

An *activity* is loosely defined as the formulation and execution of one or more actions whose result is expected to gratify the user's immediate intention. It is the unit entered into incremental interaction systems (as defined in Section 1.2.1) (Thimbleby, 1990). Entering command lines, querying databases, and locating and selecting items in a menu hierarchy are some examples. Copy typing is not: it is continuous rather than incremental, and it is not a cognitive activity (at least, not for the skilled typist).

A *recurrent system* is defined as an open-ended system in which users predominantly repeat activities they have invoked previously.[2] In other words, although many activities are possible, most (but not all) are repetitions of previous activities rather than freshly generated ones.

The fundamental notion behind recurrent systems is that activities are repeated. The frequency of repeats is called the *recurrence rate*, and it identifies the proba-

---

[1] Some of the findings in this chapter were first presented at the 1988 ACM CHI Conference on Human Factors in Computing Systems held in Washington, D.C. (Greenberg and Witten, 1988b).

[2] I first conceived the idea of recurrent systems in an earlier work (Greenberg, 1984). Originally called *repetitively accessed databases*, it concerned information retrieval of items from a database. The current term and definition subsumes the previous one.

bility that any activity is a repeat of a previous one. The *total activities* is a count of all submissions the user has entered, whereas *different activities* count only those that are different. The recurrence rate $\mathcal{R}$ over a set of user activities is calculated as:

$$\mathcal{R} = \frac{\text{total activities} - \text{different activities}}{\text{total activities}} \times 100\%$$

For a system to be classed as "recurrent," the recurrence rate may exhibit a moderate variation across users, provided that the average rate is fairly high.

Although many old activities are repeated, new ones are constantly added to the repertory. The rate at which new activities are composed and introduced to the dialog is the *composition rate* C:

$$C = \frac{\text{different activities}}{\text{total activities}} \times 100\% = 100 - \mathcal{R}$$

Activity formation within recurrent systems is open-ended, as there are a very large number of possible activities available. A *dynamic* recurrent system is one that incorporates new activities regularly. They are *static* when C is close to zero (e.g., using commands, Chapter 3). Even when new activities are constantly generated, only a small subset of the possibilities could be selected by any one user.

One purpose of this chapter is to clarify further what a recurrent system is. A few systems that fit the definition given in this section are studied and their common properties extracted. To start with, command use is obviously a recurrent system. It seems reasonable to suggest that the findings reported in Chapter 3 are also properties of recurrent systems. First, the set of activities invoked by any particular user is typically a small subset of the activities usually available. Second, the set of activities invoked may be disjointed or overlapping for different users of the system. Finally, different people may repeat common activities at different rates, and particular activities may be repeated by the same user at very different rates. The frequency distribution of activity selection is not expected to be uniform.

This definition and list of properties is not a strong one, for the boundary between recurrent and non-recurrent systems is not distinguished. Such a boundary specification, even a "fuzzy" one, would be subjective and would also depend upon other aspects of the system being investigated. For example, time between recurrences might be a consideration, where only short-term recurrences are counted but those repeated only after long intervals are considered different. Still, the properties provide a reasonable checklist for judging whether particular systems have potential for reuse.

It would seem that, at least on the surface, recurrent systems are just a weaker way of denoting patterns of behavior already well described by Zipf's law. However, major differences exist. First, many human-oriented observations characterized by Zipf's law are based upon cumulative results of the population. One study, for example, examined the statistics of all terms used to retrieve items over all users of two separate bibliographic databases, and describes how they conform to Zipf's law (Bennett, 1975). Similar large-scale statistics have been applied to many facets of library science (a list is given by Peachey, Bunt, and Colbourn, 1982). Yet there is no evidence that the same distribution applies to individuals. Recurrent systems, on the other hand, are centered around the statistics of activities of individuals, rather than large groups. Second, Zipf's law typically deals with very large numbers, and tends to break down with few observations (see Bennett, 1975 for one example). Recurrent systems are quite comfortable with small numbers. As will be seen, patterns within some recurrent systems may be identified by observing a sequence of less than one hundred actions performed by one individual (see Section 5.2.1).

5.2 Recurrent systems in the non-computer world

Are recurrent systems just artifacts peculiar to computer use, or are they everyday phenomena in the natural world? This section suggests the latter. Without belaboring the point, a few natural and reasonable possibilities follow.

- A cookbook has a subset of recipes referred to repeatedly by a single homemaker. However, usage patterns differ because not all people favor the same recipes. Some cooks prefer tried-and-true recipes, and thus will use a small set of recipes many times. Others desire variety and select from a larger recipe set with less repetition. A similar analogy may be made to selections from a book of verse, readings in the Bible, or sections and columns read in a newspaper.
- An audiophile listens to different records repeatedly. Some are heard more than others, and new styles come into favor while old ones fall out.
- Within tool-oriented contexts, tradespeople and artisans use some tools more often than others.
- Procedures carried out by most office workers are routine. Still, special procedures are sometimes followed for rarer conditions and exceptions, and new ones are created to handle unexpected situations.

Empirical evidence supports the existence of recurrent systems in a variety of task domains. Telephone use is one example, and our investigation is described in this section. Subsequent sections will illustrate two other examples: retrieving topics from technical manuals, and entering command lines in UNIX.

5.2.1 Telephone usage – a limited study

Telephone usage is examined as a first example of a recurrent system, where an activity is simply a number being dialed. This seems a natural choice, for we know from experience that:

Table 5.1. *Telephone usage statistics*

Measures	Results per subject				
	1	**2**	**3**	**4**	**5**
Total calls	313	129	119	106	106
Different calls	104	55	60	53	39
Recurrence rate	66.8%	57.4%	49.6%	50%	63.2%
Average recurrence rate	57.4% (std dev = 7.7)				

- many calls are to people/firms that have been called before;
- some calls are new ones that have not been made before;
- numbers are called with differing frequencies;
- usage patterns evolve slowly over time.

This section will describe a few simple analyses that determine empirically some characteristics of telephone usage as a recurrent system.

A small-scale study was conducted previously on individual telephone usage, as reported in an earlier work (Greenberg, 1984). The intent was to inspect telephone usage for patterns of recurrences in the numbers dialed. Fourteen telephone users known to the researcher were asked to keep a list of all calls originating from their office and/or home telephones. Instructions were to record consistently all completed calls they had made, including busy or wrong numbers and repeated calls. The time frame varied from one to three months. Although the original report summarized results for all subjects, the present analysis removes artifacts ascribed to subjects who had made relatively few calls. Only those five users who had made over one hundred calls are described here. Data is also reanalyzed to see how new calls are generated over time, to review the equilibrium of the apparently stable recurrence rate, and to see if the frequency distribution of recurring numbers exhibits temporal recency.

Telephone use by the top five single users was surveyed and compiled, with the results summarized in Table 5.1. The collected data was surprisingly consistent in many respects. First, new telephone numbers were dialed regularly, as indicated by the relatively smooth and seemingly linear lines in Figure 5.1. The horizontal axis represents the number of calls made, whereas the vertical axis indicates the number of different calls. This result suggests that telephone use is not restricted to a few numbers dialed repeatedly, but is, in fact, open-ended.

How many calls are recurrences of previous ones? The recurrence rate $\mathcal{R}$ calculated over all calls made by each subject is noted in Table 5.1. The average observed value over all users is about 57%.

But how stable is the recurrence rate (or, for that matter, the seemingly linear composition rate)? What is the relationship between the rate and the number of

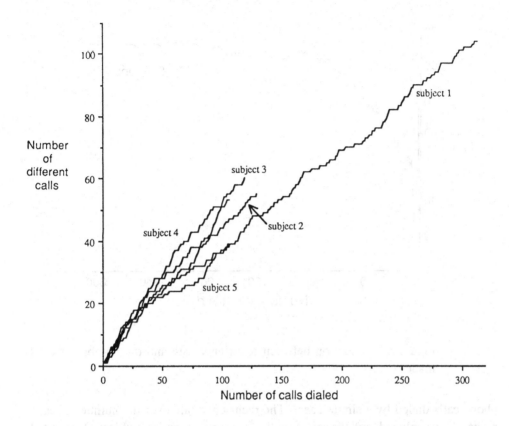

Figure 5.1. The number of different calls made vs. the number of calls dialed so far.

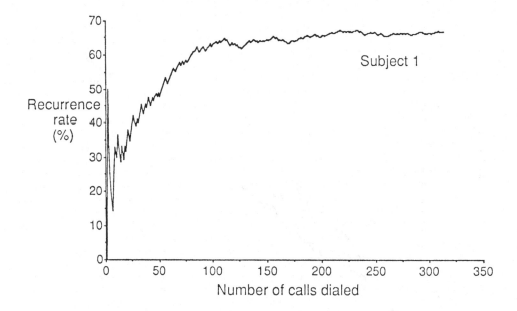

Figure 5.2. Relation between recurrence rate and the number of calls made.

phone calls dialed by a single user? The recurrence rate over the number of calls made was reanalyzed, and the result for the most prolific caller (Subject 1) is plotted in Figure 5.2.[3] The graph indicates that the rate of recurrences rises quickly over the first twenty calls and less quickly up to one hundred calls. The original report noted that $\mathcal{R}$ then seems to approach an equilibrium. However, a regression analysis made on the recurrence rate for 150 calls and over indicates a positive correlation between the rate and the number of calls dialed ($r = .661, df = 162, p << .01$), although the rate of increase is small ($slope = .012$). Because the recurrence rate $\mathcal{R}$ should equal the slope of Figure 5.1 (the composition rate $\mathcal{C}$), the trends seen there are, in fact, non-linear.

Note that the study observed people who already had established patterns of telephone use. The initial recurrence values (and their corresponding inflated composition rate) are low only because some established and highly repeated numbers are being encountered for the first time. One interpretation of the graph is that users repeat phone numbers almost immediately, as shown by the rapid initial rise. Second, some calls are probably repeated over a slightly longer period of time,

---

[3]Although the original graph in Greenberg (1984) averaged the data points over slices of ten calls, Figure 5.2 gives a true mapping of the recurrence rate up to each call. Also, only one subject is drawn here for clarity. Plots of the other subjects showed similar trends.

as revealed by the slow but steady increase in the middle of the curve. Finally, there is a near cessation of increase in the rate of recurrences after eighty calls. This indicates that although some calls are repeated over a long time period, a high number of new and rarely repeated calls are made. For example, the composition rate C was estimated at 33% for this subject (as shown in Figure 5.1). There seem to be four general categories of calls: highly popular numbers that are called quite often; moderately popular ones called infrequently; once-only calls that are never or very rarely repeated, and new ones never seen before that are incorporated in the repertory. This view agrees well with introspective expectations.

The original report also examined the frequency distribution of all calls made, by ranking each subject's calls by frequency. Of particular importance in the findings is the decreasing trend in frequency of use over the calls, indicating a diverse spectrum between highly and rarely repeated numbers. It was suggested that the same decreasing trend can be loosely modeled by the Zipf distribution, although the Zipf decrease is significantly more pronounced than in the telephone usage distribution.

Finally, telephone numbers that have just been dialed are more likely to be repeated than those dialed long ago. This notion of "temporal recency" is illustrated by the five frequency distributions, one for each subject, drawn in Figure 5.3. The method of analysis is described in Section 5.4.2. The horizontal axis represents the distance of the number about to be submitted from the position of a matching old one maintained in a temporally ordered list. The vertical axis shows the recurrence rate for particular distances. For example, 10% of Subject 1's calls are a repeat of the last call made, 8% repeat the second from last, 5% the third from last, and so on down the list. Figure 5.4 draws the same results for Subject 1 in a slightly different way – the vertical axis is now the running sum of recurrences over distance. For example, around 41% of all calls are repeats of one of the previous ten dialed. The horizontal line at the top is R (67%), which, because new calls are also composed regularly, is the limit of the running sum. The striking feature of both figures is that the last few calls are more likely to be repeated than any others.[4]

In summary, the review of this study indicates that telephone usage is a dynamic recurrent system, and adds the property that the probability of an item recurring is related to its recency of selection. However, the limited number of subjects polled over a relatively short time period does not supply enough data to support anything but general statements about usage patterns.

---

[4]Even if this distribution were uniform probability, the last few calls would still exhibit a higher frequency of recurrence, and could be misconstrued as temporal recency. However, Greenberg (1988a) shows that the artificial recency effect produced by the uniform probability distribution is far smaller than the recency effects actually observed, and can be effectively ignored.

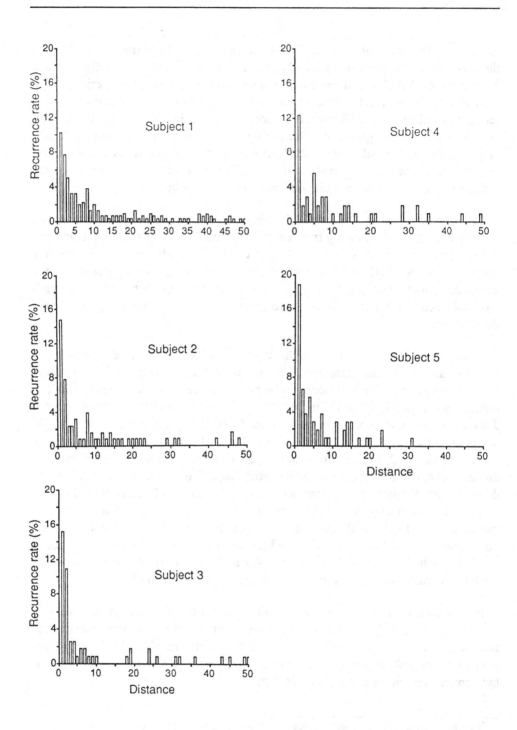

Figure 5.3. Recurrences of phone numbers as a measure of distance.

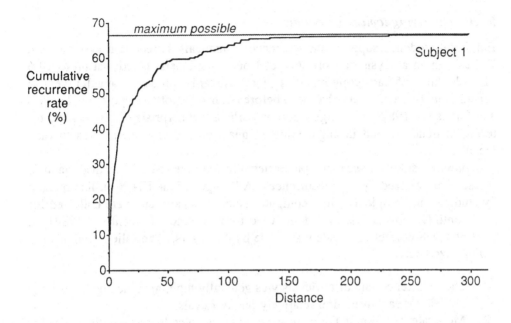

Figure 5.4. Cumulative recurrences of phone numbers as a measure of distance.

5.3 Recurrent systems in information retrieval

A second potential area of high recurrences is in information retrieval. Intuitions about the recurrence rate of such systems are perhaps not so immediate as with telephone access. Still, a few arguments for suspecting recurrences follow. First, it is usually difficult to remember particular details of information retrieved, especially if it is obscure, technical, or numerical in nature. Retrieval recurrences over short time periods are therefore likely, because details of a document require constant reviewing. Second, different information fragments are not sought equally. People may recall "important" information fragments repeatedly over long time periods. Finally, previously acquired information may become stale. As information is rarely static, the same question may be posed repeatedly and the answer checked for changes. Airline arrival and departure information available through teletext environments is one example of dynamic information. Another example is the slowly changing standards described in technical manuals, which become obsolete over time.

This section reviews how people retrieve topics in one type of information system – technical manuals.

5.3.1   *Retrieving topics in manuals*

Empirical evidence supports the existence of manuals as recurrent systems. M. E. Lesk, in an analysis of work logs of Boeing engineers, noted that up to 70% of all lookups of hard copy manuals (e.g., standards, product manuals) were to specific things the engineers had seen before but had forgotten (reported in Dumais and Landauer, 1982). The high figure is perhaps not surprising in retrospect, for technical details found in engineering manuals do not lend themselves to easy recall.

A previous study shows that topic retrieval in computer-based technical manuals is also characterized by high recurrences. All usages of the UNIX on-line manual by students and employees in a computer science department were collected for one month (Bramwell, 1983) and analyzed for recurrences (Greenberg, 1984). A total of 4,978 correct retrievals was made by 443 users. The salient findings are summarized here.

1. The recurrence rate of retrievals was generally high, approaching an average of 50% for each user after relatively few retrievals.
2. Moderate variation in the recurrence rate was noted between individuals. For example, users who had made between 17 and 19 retrievals had a standard deviation of 17.1% over the average rate of 45.2%. Extremes were 12% and 71%.
3. Each user retrieved only a small subset of the topics available.
4. Few common retrievals were noted between users, even when user tasks were similar.
5. The frequency distribution of the topics retrieved by an individual varied substantially from user to user. Although no uniform distribution was noted, the general trend was to access most topics between one and three times, with a smaller set being called on more often.

In general, one can conclude that retrieving topics in technical manuals is highly repetitive. The properties of recurrent systems listed so far are also supported. It is hypothesized that these results generalize to most structured documents, such as those found in hypertext systems, and to general information retrieval facilities provided by standard databases. Further work is required to substantiate this hypothesis.

5.4   UNIX *csh* as a recurrent system

As mentioned previously, command use is certainly a recurrent system, although it is a "static" one because C is so low. A separate question is whether complete command lines submitted to general-purpose command-based environments also follow the properties of recurrent systems. If they do, what patterns do these recurrences exhibit? This section investigates statistics of command line recurrences by subjects using the UNIX *csh*.

Because commands often act on objects and are qualified with options, it is important to look at the command line as a whole (see the concluding remarks of Chapter 3). After introducing some terminology, two questions particularly relevant to reuse facilities are addressed in this section. Both concern the statistics of complete command lines entered by the user to UNIX. This is especially important, for lines are the incremental unit of *csh*. Also, reuse facilities usually simplify redoing the complete activity, rather than its isolated components. This section first examines how often a user actually repeats command lines over the course of a dialog. Particular attention is paid to the variation in this rate between groups and between individuals, and its stability over the number of command lines entered. Second, the probability that the next command line will match a user's previous input is described. This is measured as a function of the number of entries that have elapsed since that input.

In the following discussion, a *command line* is a single complete line (up to a terminating carriage return) entered by the user. This is a natural unit because commands are interpreted by the system only when the return key is typed, and the complete line is a more detailed reflection of one's activity than just the command itself. Command lines typically comprise an action (the command), an object (e.g., files, strings), and modifiers (options). A sequential record of command lines entered by a user over time, ignoring boundaries between login sessions, is known as a *history list*. Erroneous submissions noticed by *csh* are not included. Unless stated otherwise, the history list is a true sequential record of every single command line typed. Duplicate activities, for example, are included. The *distance* between two lines is the difference between their positions on the list. A *working set* is a small subset of items on the history list. The number of different entries in the history list is the command line *vocabulary*. Although white space is ignored, syntactically different but semantically identical command lines are considered distinct.[5]

5.4.1 Recurrences of command lines

Although Section 3.3 showed that only a few commands account for all actions of a particular user, it is not known how often new command lines are formed and old ones recur. This is important, as it is the recurrence rate – the probability that the next item has been previously entered – that existing reuse facilities exploit best. One might expect that command lines would recur infrequently, given the

---

[5]For example, the command lines *ls –las* and *ls –lsa* are treated as different vocabulary items, even though they mean the same thing. Although this strategy overestimates the vocabulary size, a semantic analysis was deemed too expensive for the large data set covered.

limitless possibilities and combinations of commands, modifiers, and arguments. Surprisingly, this is not the case.

I investigated how often lines are repeated by counting the command line vocabulary size. Let $t_{cmd\ lines}$ be the total number of command lines entered by the user (i.e., the size of the history list), and $v_{cmd\ lines}$ be the vocabulary size, or number of distinct items in that set. The overall recurrence rate, using this slightly different terminology, is calculated as described in Section 5.1:

$$\mathcal{R} = \frac{t_{cmd\ lines} - v_{cmd\ lines}}{t_{cmd\ lines}} \times 100\%$$

Do users extend their vocabularies continuously and uniformly over the duration of an interaction? If not, then the recurrence rate, measured locally, will change over time as the user's history list grows. Furthermore, calculating group means for $\mathcal{R}$ could be confounded by the large variation between the number of command lines each user enters, which was noted in Table 2.1. As $\mathcal{R}$ is a function of $v_{cmd\ lines}$ and $t_{cmd\ lines}$, it is necessary to investigate how the vocabulary size depends upon the actual number of commands entered. If users never extend their vocabulary after some short initialization period, little correlation with $t_{cmd\ lines}$ is expected. On the other hand, a strong correlation is likely if new command lines are composed regularly by a user.

A simple regression analysis was performed by contrasting $t_{cmd\ lines}$ and $v_{cmd\ lines}$ for each subject. The regression line is plotted in Figure 5.5a, where each point in the scattergram represents the value observed for each subject at the end of the study period. A statistically significant and strong correlation was found ($r = .918$, $df = 167$, $p < .01$). The moderate slope ($\mathcal{C} = 23\%$) of the regression line makes the correlation practically significant as well.

It seems reasonable from the scattergram of Figure 5.5a that $v_{cmd\ lines}$ increases linearly with $t_{cmd\ lines}$, indicating that the recurrence rate is independent of the actual number of lines entered. This was checked in two ways. The first was a simple regression analysis of $t_{cmd\ lines}$ with $\mathcal{R}$. The regression line is shown in Figure 5.5b. Here, each point represents the recurrence rate observed for each subject at the end of the study. A statistically significant correlation was found ($r = .253$, $df = 167$, $p < .01$), indicating that the recurrence rate increases with the number of commands entered. However, the high variance of data points around the line ($r^2 = .064$), and its low slope (0.002), makes this finding insignificant for practical purposes. Consequently, $\mathcal{R}$ is considered independent of $t_{cmd\ lines}$.

The second and perhaps more convincing way of observing the independence of the recurrence rate is by examining in detail the vocabulary growth of individuals. The formation of new command lines is surprisingly linear and regular, as illustrated by Figure 5.6. Similar to Figure 3.2, and using the same typical users, the horizontal axis still represents the number of lines entered so far, but now the vertical axis indicates the size of the command line vocabulary. For example, the Scientist

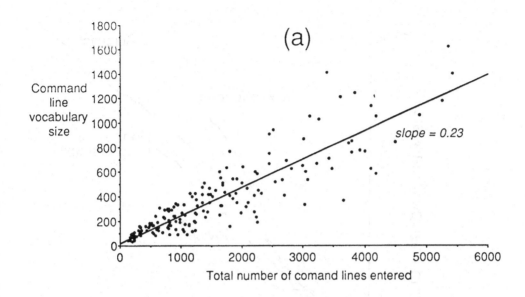

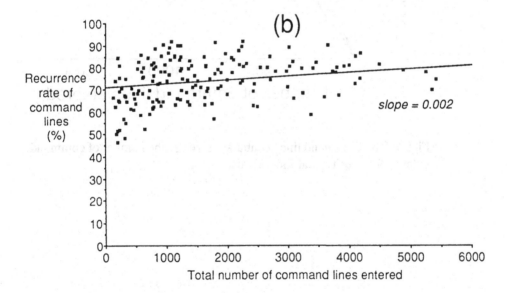

Figure 5.5. Regression: (a) command line vocabulary size; and (b) the % recurrence rate vs. the total command lines entered by each subject.

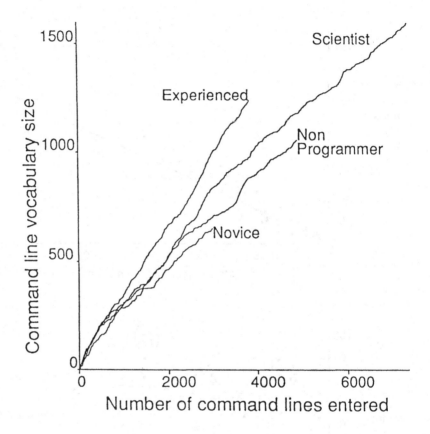

Figure 5.6. Command line vocabulary size vs. the number of commands entered for four typical individuals.

Table 5.2. *The average recurrence rate of the four sample UNIX user groups*

Sample name	Recurrence rate		Range	
	mean	std dev	minimum	maximum
Novice Programmers	80.4%	7.2	64.7%	91.7%
Experienced Programmers	74.4%	9.7	51.4%	90.0%
Computer Scientists	67.7%	8.2	46.4%	82.0%
Non-programmers	69.4%	8.1	50%	84.3%
Total	73.8%	9.6	46.4%	91.7%

subject has composed close to 1,400 new command lines after 6,000 lines were entered. The long periods of quiescence and the flurries of new activity seen in Figure 3.2 are notably absent from Figure 5.6.

Table 5.2 lists the mean recurrence rate, standard deviation, and ranges of $\mathcal{R}$ for each subject group. An analysis of variance of raw scores rejects the null hypothesis that these means are equal ($F(3, 164) = 21.42, p < .01$). The Fisher PLSD multiple comparison test suggests that all differences between group means are significant ($p < .01$), except for the Non-programmers versus Scientists. As the table indicates, the mean recurrence rate for the groups ranges between 68% and 80%, with Novice Programmers exhibiting the highest scores.

Although recurrence rate depends upon user category, and very slightly on the number of command lines entered, it is reasonable to simplify this descriptive statistic by assuming the mean $\mathcal{R}$ over all users to be 75% and $\mathcal{C}$ of 25%, independent of $t_{cmd\ lines}$. In other words, an average of three out of every four command lines entered by the user already exists on the history list. Conversely, an average of one out of every four command lines appears for the first time.

5.4.2 Command line frequency as a function of distance

For any command line entered by a user, the probability that it has been entered previously is quite high. But how do previous items contribute to this probability? Do all items on the history list have a uniform probability of recurring, or do the most recently entered submissions skew the distribution? If a graphical history mechanism displayed the previous p entries as a list (e.g., HISTMENU, Bobrow, 1986), what is the probability that this includes the next entry?

The recurrence distribution as a measure of distance was calculated for each user. First, let $\mathcal{R}_{s,d}$ be the recurrence rate at a given distance for a single person, obtained by processing each subject's data. Figure 5.7 shows the algorithm used to obtain all values of $\mathcal{R}_{s,d}$ from a subject's trace. The mean recurrence rate for a

Given:
- a trace numbered from 1 through n, where n is the last line entered;
- an array of counters used to accumulate the number of recurrences at a particular distance.

Algorithm:

```
/* For each item, find its nearest match on the history list and record it */
for (i := 1 to n)
        for (j := i–1 downto 1)
                if (submissionᵢ = submissionⱼ) then begin
                        distance := i–j;
                        counter[distance] := counter[distance] + 1;
                        break; /* jump out of inner loop */
                end
/* The averaged value found in each counter is ℛₛ,d */
for (distance := 1 to n)
        counter[distance] := (counter[distance]/n) * 100;
```

Figure 5.7. Processing a subject's trace for all values of $\mathcal{R}_{s,d}$.

given distance d over all S subjects in a particular group is then calculated as:

$$\mathcal{R}_d = \frac{1}{S}\sum_{s=1}^{S}\mathcal{R}_{s,d}$$

These group means are plotted in Figure 5.8a. The vertical axis represents $\mathcal{R}_d$, the rate of command line recurrences, whereas the horizontal axis shows the position of the repeated command line on the history list relative to the current one. The slight distortional effects of the uniform probability distribution are ignored. Taking Novice Programmers, for example, there is a $\mathcal{R}_{d1} = 11\%$ probability that the current command line is a repeat of the previous entry (distance $= 1$), $\mathcal{R}_{d2} = 28\%$ for a distance of two, $\mathcal{R}_{d3} = 9\%$ for three, and so on. The most striking feature of the figure is the extreme recency of the distribution.

The previous seven or so inputs contribute the majority of recurrences. Surprisingly, it is not the last but the second-to-last command line that dominates the distribution. The first and third are roughly the same, whereas the fourth through seventh give small but significant contributions. Although the probability values of $\mathcal{R}_d$ continually decrease after the second item, the rate of decrease and the low values make all distances beyond the previous ten items equivalent for practical purposes. This is illustrated further in Figure 5.8b, which plots the same data for the grouped total as a running sum of the probability over a wider range of distances. The running sum of the recurrence rate up to a given distance D for a single person is called $\mathcal{R}_D$. Its mean value over a group of subjects is calculated as

$$\mathcal{R}_D = \frac{1}{S}\sum_{s=1}^{S}\sum_{d=1}^{D}\mathcal{R}_{s,d}$$

The most recently entered command lines on the history list are responsible for most of the cumulative probabilities. For example, there is a $\mathcal{R}_{D_{10}} = 47\%$ chance that the next submission will match a member of a working set containing the ten previous submissions. In comparison, all further contributions are slight (although their sum total is not). The horizontal line at the top represents a ceiling to the recurrence rate, as $C = 26\%$ of all command lines entered are first occurrences.

Figure 5.8a also shows that the differing recurrence rates between user groups, noted previously in Table 5.2, are mostly attributed to the three previous command lines. Recurrence rates are practically identical elsewhere in the distribution. This difference is strongest on the second to last input, with the probability ranging from a low of 10% for Scientists to a high of 28% for Novice Programmers.

5.5 Concluding remarks

This chapter introduced the notion of recurrent systems and provided empirical evidence of their existence in both natural and computer domains. The three

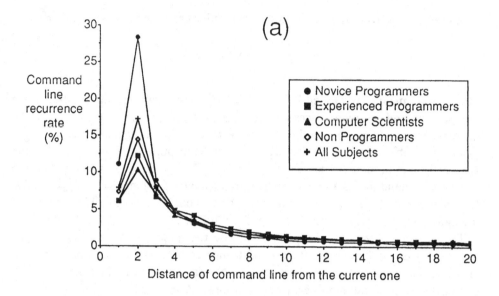

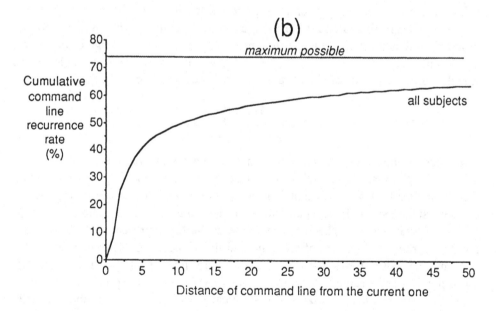

Figure 5.8. (a) Recurrence distribution; and (b) cumulative recurrence distribution as a measure of distance.

diverse examples studied – telephone usage, information retrieval, and command line interfaces – show remarkable similarity in the way activities are repeated. All satisfy the (admittedly vague) definition of recurrent systems set out in Section 5.1. A few common properties of recurrent systems were also stated.

The statistics of UNIX *csh* use, and to a lesser extent telephone dialing, indicate that the most recently submitted activities are the most likely to be repeated. These statistics confirm the potential of reuse facilities in general, and verify the assumptions of recency made by history mechanisms.

Four major weaknesses and criticisms of the idea of recurrent systems and the empirical studies reported in this chapter are noted below. First, the definition of recurrent systems is not precise, as no benchmark values are indicated. This is intentional, because any values provided would be ad hoc (although observed values for $\mathcal{R}$ seem to range from 40%–80%).

Second, the study of telephone usage is very limited. More subjects are necessary and a longer observation period is required, especially considering the initial instability of $\mathcal{R}$ over the first one hundred calls. A more rigorous method for recording calls is required as well. Although subjects say they were diligent in recording all calls, there was no way to ascertain that they actually did. Also, other factors should be included in the analysis. For example, what is the effect on the patterns of calls made by teenagers versus adults? What about business versus personal calls?

Third, the study of manual usage is very limited. Although many subjects were available, the relatively small values and the high variance in topic retrievals by subjects make it difficult to determine statistically significant patterns.

Fourth, undue attention may be paid to recency. Are there better methods for predicting a user's next activity? The next chapter tackles this question.

Finally, traces of subjects' activities in all three studies were not annotated. Why do people actually repeat activities? Although this chapter observed that they do, we can only make educated guesses as to the reasons behind their actions.

6

Reuse opportunities in UNIX csh – potential and actual

In this chapter, I consider the potential and actual reuse opportunities within UNIX. First, several methods are suggested that could increase the likelihood that the next submission matches an item in a small set of predictions offered to the user for review and reuse. All methods are applied to the UNIX traces, and the predictive "quality" of each method is measured and contrasted against the others. In the second part of the chapter, I investigate how well the reuse facilities supplied by the UNIX shell are used in practice.

6.1   Conditioning the distribution

In the last chapter, particular attention was paid to the recurrence of command lines during *csh* use, and to the probability distribution of the next line given a sequential history list of previous ones. We saw that the most striking feature of the collected statistics is the tremendous potential for a historical reuse facility: the recurrence rate is high and the last few submissions are the likeliest to be repeated.

One may predict what the user will do next by looking at those recent submissions. But there is still room for improvement, because a significant portion of recurrences are *not* recent submissions. Can better predictions of the user's next step be offered? This section proposes and evaluates alternative models of arranging a user's command line history that will condition the distribution in different ways.

The recurrence distributions of Section 5.4.2 were derived by considering all input for a user as one long sequential stream, with no barriers placed between sessions. We have seen that although a small set of recently entered command lines accounts for a high portion of repetitions, many others lie outside. Consider a working set of the ten previous items on the history list. From Figure 5.8b, there is a $C = 26\%$ chance that the next command line has not appeared before, a $\mathcal{R}_{D_{10}} = 47\%$ chance that it has occurred within the working set, and a 27% chance that it last appeared further back. This section explores the possibility that the distribution can be conditioned, first to increase the recurrence probabilities over a working set of a given size, and second to improve the overall "quality" of predictions offered. The following subsections explain how quality is assessed, describe a variety of conditioning techniques, and apply these conditions to the traces that have been collected.

6.1.1 The quality of predictions

Predictions of activities for reuse are only effective when the search for and selection of an offering is less work for the user than submitting it afresh. Work is therefore used to measure prediction quality. The smaller the amount of work required for reuse as opposed to resubmission, the higher the quality of the set of predictions offered. The selection of a high-quality prediction either reduces the cognitive effort of reconstructing the original activity or minimizes the physical work required to enter that activity to the system.

The metric for work introduced here is called M_D, and comprises two components that estimate a prediction's quality. The first is $\mathcal{R}_D$, the probability that the desired item appears on a displayed list of length $p = D$. Its calculation was given in Section 5.4.2. The second, called $\bar{c}_d$, is the average number of characters saved by reusing the matching activities at exactly a particular distance d. Incorporating string length as a partial indicator of work assumes, of course, that longer strings are harder to recall and reenter than short ones. M_D indicates the average number of characters saved over all submissions when repeated activities are selected from a list of candidates of length D. By using M_D, predictive methods can be numerically compared and ranked accordingly.

The calculation of M_D and its components proceeds as follows. First, let $\bar{c}_{s,d}$ be the average number of characters saved by a subject s per recurrence at distance d, calculated as:

$$\bar{c}_{s,d} = \frac{c_{s,d}}{r_{s,d}}.$$

The term $c_{s,d}$ is the total number of characters saved by the subject reusing all matching recurrences at a particular distance, and $r_{s,d}$ is the number of matching recurrences at that distance. When $\bar{c}_{s,d}$ is averaged over all subjects S, we get $\bar{c}_d$, calculated as:

$$\bar{c}_d = \frac{1}{S}\sum_{s=1}^{S}\bar{c}_{s,d}.$$

But $\bar{c}_d$ just gives the average characters saved by using a correct prediction at a particular distance. An alternative approach calculates M_d, which includes the probability that the prediction is correct. More specifically, M_d is the mean number of characters saved at a particular distance over all subjects:

$$M_d = \frac{1}{S}\sum_{s=1}^{S}\bar{c}_{s,d}\mathcal{R}_{s,d},$$

where $\mathcal{R}_{s,d}$ is a particular subject's probability of a recurrence at the given distance, defined in Section 5.4.2 . Note that M_d differs from $\bar{c}_d$ as it is the average savings *per submission* rather than per recurrence. The final step in calculating M_D shows the cumulative average savings in characters per submission when all D predictions are available for selection:

$$M_D = \sum_{d=1}^{D} M_d = M_1 + M_2 + \ldots + M_{d=D}.$$

Both $\mathcal{R}_D$ and M_D will be used in this chapter as metrics for evaluating working sets of particular sizes, although values of $\mathcal{R}_d$ (Section 5.4.2) and $\bar{c}_d$ are included for reference.

6.1.2   Different conditioning methods

A variety of conditioning methods are described here. These include not only conditions that are expected to perform quite well, but also weak ones that have been implemented in existing reuse facilities. For each method I indicate how the recorded data will be analyzed to assess its effectiveness. The algorithms used to find $\mathcal{R}_{s,d}$ for each case are not elaborated (they are minor variations of the one shown in Figure 5.7). Results are presented in the next section and show how effective – or ineffective – these conditioning methods really are.

Sequential ordering by recency. This conditioning method was described in the previous chapter, and is simply a time-ordered list of all submissions entered by the user. The first column of Table 6.1 illustrates the sequentially ordered history list numbered by order of entry. The most recent submission appears on the top, and the history list – as with all other examples on the table – is intended to be reviewed top-down.

There are two virtues of recency. First, the items presented would be the ones a user has just entered and still remembers. The user knows they are on the list without having to scan through it. Second, unlike some adaptive methods, there is no initial startup instability of deciding what to present when only a few items are available.

Pruning duplicates from the history list. The sequentially ordered history lists mentioned so far maintain a record of every single command line typed. Duplicate lines are not pruned off the list. On a history list of limited length, duplicates occupy space that could be used more fruitfully by other command lines.

There are two obvious strategies for pruning redundancies, as described by Barnes and Bovey (1986). The first saves the activity in its original location on the history list (as in HYPERCARD's *recent* facility, (Section 4.1.4) whereas the second saves it in its latest position (as in WINDOW MANAGEMENT WINDOW, Section 4.1.2). It is expected that the latter approach would give better performance, because not only is local context maintained, but unique and low-probability command

Table 6.1. *Examples of history lists conditioned by different methods*

Sequential		Duplicates removed				Frequency order				
starting in ~/text		*original position*		*latest position*		*secondary key is recency*			*secondary key is reverse-recency*	
14	cd ~/figs	12	cd ~/text	14	cd ~/figs	10	ls	3	10	ls	3
13	print draft	9	graph fig1	13	print draft	14	cd ~/figs	2	4	edit draft	2
12	cd ~/text	8	edit fig2	12	cd ~/text	13	print draft	2	11	edit fig1	2
11	edit fig1	7	edit fig1	11	edit fig1	11	edit fig1	2	13	print draft	2
10	ls	5	cd ~/figs	10	ls	4	edit draft	2	14	cd ~/figs	2
9	graph fig1	3	print draft	9	graph fig1	12	cd ~/text	1	8	edit fig2	1
8	edit fig2	2	edit draft	8	edit fig2	9	graph fig1	1	9	graph fig1	1
7	edit fig1	1	ls	4	edit draft	8	edit fig2	1	12	cd ~/text	1
6	ls										
5	cd ~/figs										
4	edit draft										
3	print draft										
2	edit draft										
1	ls										

Alphabetic		Directory sensitive				Commands	
duplicates removed		*directory context is ~/text*		*directory context is ~/figs*		*recency, no duplicates*	
14	cd ~/figs	14	cd ~/figs	12	cd ~/text	14	cd
12	cd ~/text	3	print draft	8	edit fig1	13	print
4	edit draft	5	cd ~/figs	10	ls	11	edit
11	edit fig1	4	edit draft	9	graph fig1	10	ls
8	edit fig2	13	print draft	11	edit fig2	9	graph
9	graph fig1	2	edit draft	7	edit fig1		
10	ls	1	ls	6	ls		
13	print draft						

with duplicates removed, events saved in latest position			
1	ls	8	edit fig2
4	edit draft	9	graph fig1
13	print draft	10	ls
14	cd ~/figs	11	edit fig1
		12	cd ~/text

Note: In UNIX, users change directories through the *cd* command. The "~" is shorthand for the home directory. Following "/"'s indicate sub–directories.

entries will migrate to the back of the list over time.[1]

Consider, for example, the two pruned event lists in the second major column of Table 6.1. Both are the same length, which is considerably shorter than the plain sequential one in the first column. But the order of entries is quite different. Even in this short list, the disadvantage of saving items in their original position is evident. Local context is weak (indicated by the scattered event numbers), and the frequently used *ls* command line is poorly positioned at the bottom of the list.

Data sets are reanalyzed using both strategies of pruning duplicates from sequential history lists, where recurring items are either kept in their original position or moved to their latest position.

Frequency ordering. Perhaps the most obvious way of ranking activities is by frequency, where the most often-used command line appears at the front of the history list and the rarest one at the end. This approach is conservative. Old and frequently used items tend to stay around – unless there is a built-in decay factor – whereas newer submissions will not appear near the head of the list until they are repeated as often as the old ones. Still, frequency ordering may do as well as or perhaps even better than recency.

Although ordering items by frequency is straightforward, it is not clear how to sort items of identical frequencies. One possibility uses recency as the secondary sorting key. For example, if the current submission is a recurrence, its frequency count is increased by 1 and it is relocated before all other recurrences with the same count. Another approach uses a secondary sort-by-reverse-recency, where the recurring item is placed at the tail of the list of items with identical frequencies. Contrasting these two methods gives a bound to the range of recency effects. Examples of each are shown in Table 6.1, where the number to each item's right counts how often that line has been submitted.

It is expected that frequency ordering may do quite well, given that UNIX command lines often consist of a frequently executed command without arguments. But probably fewer characters are predicted, because short lines would tend to dominate the higher frequencies. Another disadvantage of frequency ordering is that counts must now be associated with every submission. At best, this just takes up some space and a little CPU time, which matters little in these days of cheap memory and fast machines. At worst, the derived probabilities associated with a young history list are quite unstable and may lead to very poor initial predictions, which could discourage a new user from placing their faith in it (cf. recency).

The data sets are analyzed by ordering history lists by frequency and using two

---

[1]Saving recurrencing activities in their latest position only is equivalent to "self-organized files," where successfully located records are moved to the beginning of the sequentially accessed file. As briefly discussed by Knuth (1973), often-used items tend to be located near the beginning of the file, and the average number of comparisons is always less than twice the optimal value possible.

cases of secondary sorting: recency and reverse-recency. Because there is no advantage in keeping multiple copies of command lines, they are pruned from the list.

Alphabetic ordering. Sorting activities alphabetically is another possibility. Although items on alphabetic ordered lists are best found by binary search or pattern matching, surprisingly many systems provide only scrolling capabilities for sequential searching. One example is the *window management window*, described in Section 4.1.2, which provides it as a display option (Barnes and Bovey, 1986). We would expect poor performance of a distribution derived from alphabetic ordering. Letter frequencies aside, it should do no better than a random ordering of events. Performance is easily evaluated by seeing how many pages of previous activities would have to be scrolled on average before the desired item is found.

User's traces were reanalyzed by placing their command lines on a history list in ASCII order. If a new submission is identical to one already on the list, it is ignored. An example of an ASCII-ordered list is included in Table 6.1.

Context-sensitive history lists by directory. Users of computer systems perform much task switching (Bannon, Cypher, Greenspan, and Monty, 1983), where each task represents an independent or interacting context. (See Section 8.1 for further discussion.) Because many command line submissions are specific to the task at hand, it is reasonable to hypothesize that context-sensitive history lists will give better local predictions.

Ideally, the reuse facility would infer the context of every submission entered and place it on an appropriate history list, creating a new one if needed. Events common to multiple contexts could perhaps be shared between lists. The system would then infer the likely context of the next submission and offer its predictions for reuse only from the appropriate list.

Associating users' activities with their tasks or goals is not easy, and such inferences cannot be made reliably. Instead, a simple heuristic provides a reasonable guess of the true contexts. UNIX furnishes a hierarchical directory system for maintaining files. As many user actions reference these files, I hypothesize that the current working directory defines a context for command lines. This grouping of command lines by the current directory (or perhaps by the obvious alternative of windows) is just an estimate – possibly a poor one – of actual task contexts.

When data was collected, each user submission was annotated with the directory it was run in. The traces were reanalyzed by creating a new history list for each new directory visited and placing the command line on that list. The recurrence distance for each submission was then calculated by retrieving the history list for the current directory of the next submission and searching it for the most recent match.

The second main column in the lower half of Table 6.1 illustrates the directory-sensitive condition applied to the sequential input, where each sub-column is sensitive to a particular directory. Most command lines refer to files in that directory, and would rarely be used in other directories. Some command lines, however, are common to more than one directory (for example, *ls* for listing files).

Ordering commands by recency. Chapter 3 showed that most individuals use few commands, and that the frequency distribution of command selection is very uneven. It would be interesting to see how a history list comprised of recency-ordered commands (not command lines) would perform. Although we expect the probability of a matching prediction $\mathcal{R}_D$ to be quite high, the characters predicted per recurrence would be lower, because the rest of the command line is ignored (see the example in Table 6.1).

User traces are reanalyzed over history lists of commands. Duplicate commands are pruned, with a single copy of the command kept in its position of latest occurrence.

Partial matches. Instead of the next command line matching a previous one exactly, partial matching may be allowed. This is helpful when people make simple spelling mistakes, when the same command and options are invoked on different arguments, when command lines are extended, and so on.

However, the potential benefit is highly user and situation dependent, for the user must alter the selected sequence before it is invoked. Consider the next submission *s* and its partial match to a previous event *e* on the history list. If selecting and modifying *e* is easier and more reliable than entering *s*, then it is an attractive strategy. If *s* is long, for example, and differs from *e* by a single character, selecting and fixing *e* is probably faster. If *s* is short, it is unlikely that the user would bother.

The possibility of the given pattern retrieving an undesired interposed event must be considered too. Consider, for example, a user who wishes to invoke the document formatter *roff* on the file *file.n* after submitting the following *csh* input lines.

$$roff\ file.n$$
$$rm\ *.n$$
$$edit\ file.n$$

The user enters the *csh* reuse directive *!r*, which recalls the last event beginning with the letter r, and mistakenly executes *rm *.n* instead of *roff file.n*. All files ending with *.n are removed, and the work is lost.

Partial matches by prefix were investigated. Command lines are matched whenever it is a prefix of the next submission. If *s* = "*edit fig2*," for example, some partial matches on prefix for *e* could be "*ed*," "*edit*," "*edit fig*," and "*edit fig2*."

In partial matching, history lists are not altered. Rather, it is the definition of recurrence that has changed. Any increase in predictive probability comes at the expense of fewer useful characters predicted. Effects of partial matching are shown for a recency-ordered history list both with duplicates retained and with duplicates pruned.

A hierarchy of command lines and command-sensitive sub-lists. One way of increasing the effectiveness of a history list is by using existing items on the display as a hierarchical entry point to related items. More specifically, consider a history list of command lines where each item can further raise a secondary list of all lines that share the same initial command (called a command-sensitive list). One first scans down i entries in the normal list for either an exact match that terminates the search, or for a line that starts with the desired command. In the later case, the command-sensitive list is displayed (perhaps as a pop-up menu) and the search continues until an exact match is found j entries later. The distance of a matching recurrence is simply $i + j$. Given the sequential list in Table 6.1, for example, the command sensitive sub-list on item 11 would be *edit fig1*, *edit fig2*, and *edit draft*.

Such a scheme could do no worse than the original method of displaying the history list, and it has the potential to do much better. This method was tested by using recency-ordering of both the primary and command-sensitive history lists with duplicates saved in their latest position only.

Combinations. These strategies are not mutually exclusive, and they can be combined in a variety of ways. The bottom half of column 2 of Table 6.1 shows one such possibility, where the event list is conditioned by directory sensitivity and pruning. Data sets were reanalyzed using combinations of a few conditions mentioned in this section.

6.1.3 *Evaluating the conditioning methods*

Data selection. Conditioning by directory context is no different from standard sequential history if subjects work only within a single directory. Because not all subjects used multiple directories, this portion of the analysis was restricted to the Experienced Programmers, each of whom used several directories.[2] All other groups had subjects who used one directory exclusively (17 of the 55 Novice Programmers, 6 of the 25 Non-programmers, and 2 of the 52 Computer Scientists).

Each subject is reanalyzed using the afore mentioned conditioning methods and some of their combinations for redefining both the history list and the method of determining recurrences.

---

[2] Another reason for limiting the number of subjects analyzed is more pragmatic – about four to eight hours of machine time were required to process a single condition for each group.

Length of command lines and M_D. Before delving into details of how each method performs according to the quality metric, we need to determine the best performance possible. To start, the average length of command lines is 7.58 characters, where terminating line feeds are not counted and duplicate lines are included. This was calculated by finding the average line length for each subject, and averaging those results over all subjects. These numbers will underestimate the actual characters typed, for editing sequences are not included.

Because reuse facilities can predict only lines that have been entered previously, it is important to know if recurring lines have a different average length from those appearing only once. Further analysis shows that the average length of submissions that already exist on the history list is 5.97 characters, whereas those that appear for the first time are 12.29 characters long. This is not as surprising as it might seem at first, for short lines with few arguments are usually more general-purpose (and therefore reusable) than complex lines. We would expect frequently appearing lines to be shorter than lines that are rarely or never repeated.

The maximum possible value for M_D is therefore $\mathcal{R} * 5.97/100$, for M_D is calculated over all submissions. As $\mathcal{R}$ is 74.4% for Experienced Programmers, M_D for an optimal conditioning method is 4.43 characters predicted per submission.

Results. Results for all conditions are summarized in four tables, each presenting various distributions over the last fifty items of the history list. Table 6.2 presents the percentage of the frequency of submissions recurring at a particular distance ($\mathcal{R}_d$), and Table 6.3 provides the same information as a running sum over distance ($\mathcal{R}_D$). The latter includes the total recurrence rate over the complete history list, which differs with certain conditions.[3] Figure 6.1 graphs the results of Table 6.3. As with Figure 5.8b, the horizontal axis shows the position of the repeated command line on the history list relative to the current one, whereas the vertical axis represents $\mathcal{R}_D$, the rate of accumulated command line recurrences, as a percentage.

The next two tables involve the length in characters of recurrences. Table 6.4 shows the average number of characters saved for a recurrence at a given distance (the value of $\bar{c}_d$). Table 6.5 displays the metric M_D, which shows how many characters are saved for an average submission. This value accounts for recurring and non-recurring submissions, and assumes that the user can select from D predictions. Figure 6.2 graphs the performance of each conditioning method over distance using this metric.

Standard sequential. The last chapter saw an $\mathcal{R}_{D_{10}}$ of 44.4% for the Experienced Programmer group (also in Table 6.3). The metric $M_{D_{10}}$ for the same group is 2.48 characters per submission (Table 6.5), which is 55% of the maximum value it could

---

[3]The recurrence rate differs when the way of determining matching submissions changes (partial matching, commands only) and when the history list is split into multiple lists (directory sensitivity).

Table 6.2. *Probability of a recurrence over distance for various conditioning methods*

Conditioning method	Probability of a recurrence at the given distance d in percent ($\mathcal{R}_d$) Distance													
	1	2	3	4	5	6	7	8	9	10	20	30	40	50
Recency, duplicates saved:														
always	6.12	12.29	6.71	4.83	4.12	2.94	2.36	1.97	1.66	1.40	0.59	0.32	0.21	0.16
in original position only	2.53	1.75	1.30	1.08	1.01	0.82	0.79	0.66	0.75	0.61	0.35	0.34	0.32	0.23
in latest position only	6.12	12.82	7.58	5.35	4.93	3.48	2.83	2.38	1.99	1.70	0.59	0.30	0.18	0.14
Frequency order:														
second key recency	13.13	7.95	5.24	3.98	3.37	2.83	2.47	2.11	1.79	1.56	0.73	0.49	0.26	0.20
second key reverse recency	13.16	7.74	5.16	3.84	3.20	2.74	2.38	1.91	1.73	1.53	0.74	0.44	0.24	0.16
Alphabetic order:														
duplicates removed	1.27	1.00	1.21	1.30	1.02	1.25	0.76	0.87	0.85	0.57	0.68	0.48	0.32	0.52
Directory sensitive by recency:														
duplicates included	7.46	13.61	8.20	4.89	3.50	2.73	2.06	1.67	1.52	1.22	0.44	0.28	0.15	0.12
duplicates removed	7.46	14.29	9.39	5.78	4.13	3.11	2.37	2.06	1.53	1.38	0.39	0.18	0.11	0.08
Commands only by recency:														
duplicates removed	15.36	19.87	10.89	7.05	5.75	4.09	3.11	2.56	2.21	1.81	0.64	0.28	0.16	0.14
Partial matching by recency:														
duplicates included	8.17	13.49	7.61	5.45	4.51	3.35	2.60	2.18	1.85	1.59	0.63	0.34	0.26	0.16
duplicates removed	8.17	14.07	8.60	6.07	5.34	3.89	3.06	2.64	2.26	1.92	0.65	0.33	0.23	0.18
Command hierarchy:														
recency, duplicates removed	6.12	13.89	9.35	6.60	5.56	4.03	3.19	2.70	2.26	1.83	0.52	0.22	0.13	0.09

Table 6.3. *Cumulative probabilities of a recurrence over distance for various conditioning methods*

Conditioning method	Cumulative probabilities of a recurrence up to a given distance d in percent ($\mathcal{R}_D$)														$\mathcal{R}$
	Distance														
	1	2	3	4	5	6	7	8	9	10	20	30	40	50	
Recency, duplicates saved:															
always	6.12	18.41	25.12	29.94	34.06	37.00	39.36	41.33	42.99	44.39	52.67	56.82	59.58	61.47	74.42
in original position only	2.53	4.28	5.57	6.65	7.66	8.48	9.27	9.93	10.68	11.29	15.92	19.58	22.82	26.29	74.42
in latest position only	6.12	18.94	26.52	31.87	36.80	40.28	43.11	45.48	47.47	49.17	58.98	63.51	66.00	67.67	74.42
Frequency order:															
2nd key recency	13.13	21.08	26.32	30.29	33.66	36.48	38.95	41.06	42.85	44.41	55.35	60.98	64.31	66.48	74.42
2nd key reverse recency	13.16	20.89	26.05	29.90	33.09	35.83	38.21	40.12	41.84	43.37	53.63	58.85	62.02	63.93	74.42
Alphabetic order:															
duplicates removed	1.27	2.27	3.48	4.78	5.80	7.05	7.81	8.68	9.52	10.09	16.53	21.76	25.84	30.16	74.42
Directory sensitive by recency:															
duplicates included	7.46	21.07	29.27	34.16	37.66	40.39	42.44	44.12	45.63	46.85	53.52	56.62	58.48	59.69	65.53
duplicates removed	7.46	21.75	31.15	36.93	41.06	44.18	46.54	48.60	50.13	51.51	58.80	61.56	62.93	63.74	65.53
Commands only by recency:															
duplicates removed	15.36	35.23	46.12	53.17	58.92	63.01	66.12	68.68	70.89	72.70	82.61	86.83	89.05	90.49	95.24
Partial matching by recency:															
duplicates included	8.17	21.65	29.26	34.71	39.22	42.57	45.17	47.34	49.19	50.78	60.16	64.74	67.78	69.93	84.39
duplicates removed	8.17	22.23	30.83	36.90	42.25	46.14	49.20	51.84	54.10	56.02	66.90	72.04	74.94	76.88	84.39
Command hierarchy:															
recency, dup's removed	6.12	20.01	29.36	35.96	41.52	45.56	48.74	51.44	53.71	55.54	64.81	68.38	70.17	71.21	74.42

Table 6.4. *Average number of characters saved over distance per recurrence*

| Conditioning method | The average number of characters saved over all subjects per recurrence at a given distance ($\overline{c}_d$) | | | | | | | | | | | | | |
| | Distance | | | | | | | | | | | | | |
	1	2	3	4	5	6	7	8	9	10	20	30	40	50
Recency, duplicates saved:														
always	5.94	5.04	5.31	5.57	5.79	5.61	6.11	5.84	5.64	5.51	6.26	5.39	4.83	5.78
in original position only	10.60	10.24	9.76	9.51	8.41	8.83	9.49	7.97	8.17	8.00	7.18	6.70	6.11	5.42
in latest position only	5.94	5.06	5.49	5.72	5.86	5.51	5.88	5.76	5.74	5.87	6.21	5.83	5.31	5.67
Frequency order:														
second key recency	2.57	3.94	5.34	5.76	5.30	5.58	5.17	6.10	6.45	6.50	6.91	7.61	8.73	8.94
second key reverse recency	2.60	3.93	5.35	5.65	5.10	5.56	5.30	6.19	6.08	6.38	7.31	7.58	7.30	8.15
Alphabetic order:														
duplicates removed	3.52	6.67	5.67	5.66	5.66	7.09	6.12	7.10	6.90	6.79	6.33	4.65	5.97	4.84
Directory sensitive by recency:														
duplicates included	6.47	5.70	5.62	5.95	6.24	6.08	6.56	6.14	5.61	5.69	6.08	6.17	5.23	5.08
duplicates removed	6.47	5.71	5.76	6.10	6.14	6.05	6.21	6.04	5.88	5.98	6.43	4.81	6.04	4.36
Commands only by recency:														
duplicates removed	3.25	2.68	2.82	2.96	3.08	3.00	3.07	3.05	3.06	3.15	2.96	3.05	2.78	2.98
Partial matching by recency:														
duplicates included	5.54	4.86	5.02	5.18	5.32	5.22	5.45	5.02	4.94	4.90	5.24	4.09	4.30	3.99
duplicates removed	5.54	4.87	5.18	5.25	5.38	4.99	5.14	5.02	4.99	5.11	4.65	4.27	3.84	4.00
Command hierarchy:														
recency, duplicates removed	5.94	5.36	5.85	6.11	6.15	6.23	6.02	6.11	6.30	6.48	5.91	6.33	4.44	4.37

Table 6.5. *Cumulative average number of characters saved per submission over distance*

Conditioning method	Cumulative average savings in characters of D predictions over all submissions (M_D) Distance													
	1	2	3	4	5	6	7	8	9	10	20	30	40	50
Recency, duplicates saved:														
always	0.37	0.99	1.35	1.63	1.87	2.04	2.19	2.31	2.40	2.48	2.99	3.25	3.43	3.55
in original position only	0.27	0.46	0.59	0.69	0.78	0.86	0.94	0.99	1.05	1.10	1.48	1.75	1.98	2.20
in latest position only	0.37	1.02	1.44	1.76	2.05	2.25	2.42	2.56	2.68	2.78	3.40	3.69	3.86	3.98
Frequency order:														
second key recency	0.32	0.64	0.93	1.16	1.34	1.49	1.62	1.75	1.86	1.96	2.74	3.19	3.49	3.68
second key reverse recency	0.33	0.63	0.91	1.14	1.30	1.45	1.57	1.69	1.79	1.89	2.50	2.99	3.26	3.43
Alphabetic order:														
duplicates removed	0.03	0.08	0.15	0.24	0.31	0.43	0.48	0.54	0.61	0.65	1.12	1.45	1.69	1.91
Directory sensitive by recency:														
duplicates included	0.48	1.28	1.76	2.05	2.27	2.44	2.57	2.67	2.76	2.83	3.25	3.45	3.57	3.65
duplicates removed	0.48	1.32	1.88	2.24	2.45	2.68	2.83	2.95	3.04	3.13	3.59	3.77	3.87	3.93
Commands only by recency:														
duplicates removed	0.50	1.03	1.34	1.55	1.73	1.86	1.95	2.03	2.10	2.15	2.46	2.59	2.67	2.71
Partial matching by recency:														
duplicates included	0.45	1.11	1.50	1.79	2.04	2.21	2.36	2.47	2.56	2.64	3.12	3.35	3.51	3.62
duplicates removed	0.45	1.14	1.60	1.93	2.21	2.41	2.57	2.71	2.82	2.92	3.47	3.72	3.86	3.96
Command hierarchy:														
recency, duplicates removed	0.37	1.11	1.68	2.09	2.43	2.68	2.88	3.04	3.18	3.30	3.90	4.12	4.23	4.29

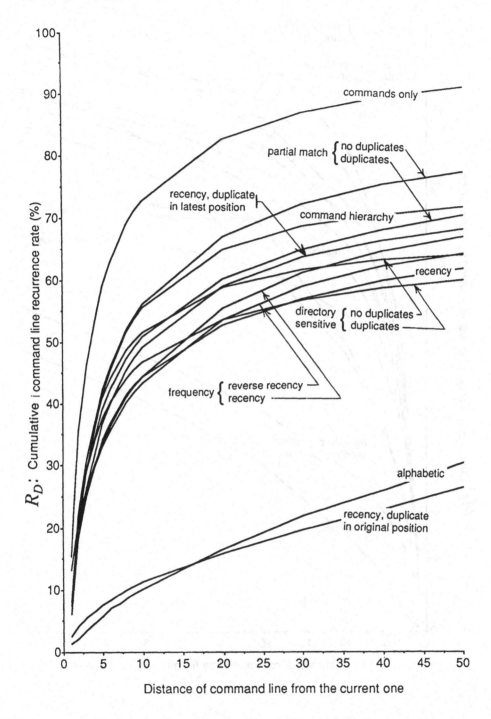

Figure 6.1. Cumulative probabilities of a recurrence over distance for various conditioning methods.

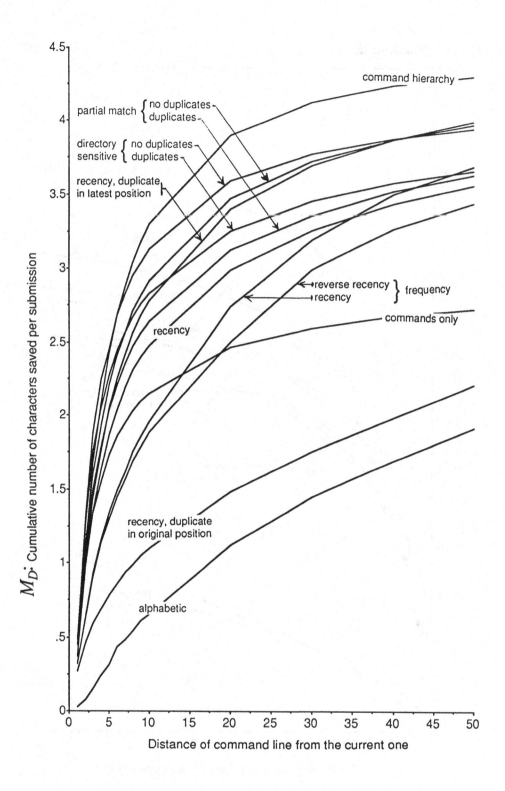

Figure 6.2. Cumulative average number of characters saved per submission over distance.

have. These figures will be used as a benchmark for comparing other conditioning methods.

Pruning duplicates. Although pruning duplicates from the history list does not alter the recurrence rate, it does shorten the total distance covered by the distribution (i.e., the history list is smaller). First, how does saving single copies of recurring activities in their original position on the history list compare with saving items in their latest position? A quick glance at the tables and graphs shows that the former gives exceedingly poor predictive performance. Curiously, saving activities in their original position gave a much higher average length of predicted strings than any other conditioning method for lines recurring over small distances (Table 6.4). But it is the low-frequency lines that must contribute most to this average, as high-frequency lines do not remain near the front of the list. This larger than expected line length supports the hypothesis that often-repeated lines are shorter on average than rarely repeated ones. The low probability values associated with those recurrences reduce any benefit accrued by predicting longer lines. Consider a ten-item working set. The probabilities $\mathcal{R}_{D_{10}}$ of a recurrence falling in that set are 11% and 49% for the original and the latest position respectively, and the corresponding values of $M_{D_{10}}$ are 1.10 and 2.78 characters per submission. Saving activities in their original position is clearly ineffective. The remainder of this book assumes that history lists with duplicates pruned will save the single copy in its position of latest occurrence.

As the working set size increases, so does the value of $\mathcal{R}_D$ associated with a duplicates-pruned list when compared to the standard sequential list (Table 6.3 and Figure 6.1). Pruning duplicates increases the overall probability of a ten-item working set by 4.8% ($\mathcal{R}_{D_{10}} = 49.1\%$ vs. 44.4%), and $M_{D_{10}}$ is increased by 0.3 characters per submission.

Frequency order. Using recency as a secondary sort in a frequency-ordered list is marginally better than sorting by reverse-recency. The overall probability of a ten-item working set is 1.1% higher, and 0.1 character more is predicted per submission. Because these values reflect the bounds of these two conditions, it is hardly worth worrying about how to do the secondary sort. Still, whenever frequency-ordered lists are discussed in the book, the better secondary sort of recency is assumed.

Frequency-ordered history lists do not do as well as strict sequential ones, even though duplicates are not included in the former. Although the probability of a hit in a ten-item working set is about the same ($\mathcal{R}_{D_{10}} = 44.4\%$), lines predicted are shorter (as expected). The metric $M_{D_{10}}$ is 0.6 characters less per submisson.

Alphabetic order. As anticipated, alphabetic ordering of history lists gives the poorest performance of any conditioning technique (this assumes sequential searching through the list). With a ten-item display, $\mathcal{R}_{D_{10}} = 10.1\%$, and only 0.65 characters are predicted per submission. If a user were scrolling through this display, a full one hundred items (or ten pages) must be reviewed on average to match $M_{D_{10}}$ for the strict sequential list!

Context-sensitive history lists by directory. Creating context-sensitive directory lists with duplicates retained decreases the overall recurrence rate for Experienced Programmers from 74.4% in the strict sequential case to 65.5%, because command lines entered in one directory are no longer available in others. Although this reduction means that plain sequential lists out-perform directory-sensitive ones over all previous entries, benefits were observed over small working sets. As Table 6.2 illustrates, the first three directory-sensitive items are more probable than their sequential counterparts, approximately equal for the fourth, and slightly less likely thereafter. The accumulated probabilities $\mathcal{R}_D$ cross over with a working set of twenty-seven items (Figure 6.1). With a working set of ten items, directory-sensitivity increases the overall probability that the next item will be in that set by 2.5% ($\mathcal{R}_{D_{10}} = 46.9\%$). The length of lines predicted in the directory-sensitive condition are also longer than those predicted by a strict sequential list, and $M_{D_{10}}$ is 0.35 character per submission higher.

Ordering commands by recency. When all aspects of a command line are ignored except for the initial command word, the recurrence rate jumps to 95.2%. The accumulated probabilities of recurrences are also very high when compared to the strict sequential list – $\mathcal{R}_{D_{10}} = 72.7\%$ vs. 44.4%. But the high predictability is offset by the low number of characters predicted. $M_{D_{10}}$ actually drops 0.3 character per prediction.

Partial matches. Pattern matching by prefix increases the recurrence rate to 84.4%, where the recurrence rate is now defined as the probability that any previous event is a prefix of the current one. Because partial matches are found before more distant (and perhaps non-existent) exact matches, an increase is expected in the rate of growth of the cumulative probability distribution. This increase is illustrated in Table 6.3 and Figure 6.1. Conditioning by partial matching increases $\mathcal{R}_{D_{10}}$ of a ten-item working set by 6.4% when compared to a strict sequential list (Table 6.3), although lines predicted are shorter (Table 6.4). Still, $M_{D_{10}}$ is increased slightly by 0.16 character per submission.

A hierarchy of command lines and command-sensitive sub-lists. The history list comprised of recency-ordered non-duplicated lines and command-sensitive sub-lists shows the best performance of all conditions evaluated. The accumulated probability of a ten-item display is $\mathcal{R}_{D_{10}} = 55.5\%$ out of the 74.4% possible. $M_{D_{10}}$ is 3.3 characters per submission, compared to the 4.4–character maximum for an optimal system.

Combinations. When conditioning methods are combined, the effects are slightly less than additive. A few possible combinations are included by removing duplicates from both the directory-sensitive and partial matching conditions. Each improves as expected, as illustrated by Tables 6.2 through 6.5 and Figures 6.1 and 6.2. Where feasible, conditioning methods can be combined even further. For example, a partially matched, pruned, and directory-sensitive history mechanism increases $\mathcal{R}_{D_{10}}$ over a strict sequential one by 12.7% with a working set of ten items (reported in Greenberg and Witten, 1988b).

6.1.4 Discussion

The recurrence rate $\mathcal{R}$ provides a theoretical ceiling on the performance of a reuse facility using literal matches. It is reached only if one reuses old submissions at every opportunity. However, finding and selecting items for reuse could well be more work than entering it afresh, especially if it is necessary to search the complete history list. Pragmatic considerations mean that most reuse facilities choose a small set of previous submissions as predictions, and offer only those for reuse. Although the last chapter demonstrated that temporal recency is a reasonable predictor, the conditioning methods described and evaluated here proved that a few simple strategies can increase predictive power even further.

We saw that up to 55% of all user activity can be successfully predicted with working sets of ten predictions for literal matches, depending upon the conditioning method chosen. Given that $\mathcal{R} = 75\%$ on average, which is the best a perfect literal reuse facility could do, this means that the best predictive method described here is about 75% effective, at least potentially.

When the quality metric is incorporated, we observe that the best method correctly predicts 3.3 characters per submission (with a working set of ten items), compared to the 4.4–character optimum calculated previously. Again, the method is about 75% effective.

In marked contrast, a few conditioning methods perform poorly. Saving duplicates in their original position has no benefit, and alphabetic ordering of the history list is questionable. Although frequency ordering does not fare badly, other methods give better results.

There is no guarantee that any of the conditioning methods described here will be effective in practice, for the cognitive and mechanical work required for finding and selecting items for reuse from even a small list may still be too costly. Research is required in three areas. First, other conditioning methods should be explored that further increase the probability of a set of predictions (up to the value of $\mathcal{R}$). One candidate could use a model similar to that used by the REACTIVE KEYBOARD (Darragh, 1988) (Section 4.2.2). Second, the size of the working set should be reduced. Ideally, only one correct prediction will be suggested. Third, the cognitive effort required for reviewing a particular conditioned set of

Table 6.6. *How history was used by the sample groups*

Sample Name	Users of history actual	%	Mean rate of using history %
Novice Programmers	11/55	20%	2.03
Experienced Programmers	33/36	92%	4.23
Computer Scientists	37/52	71%	4.04
Non-programmers	9/25	36%	4.35
Total	90/168	54%	3.89

predictions must be evaluated. One factor is whether the user knows beforehand if the item being sought appears in the set; otherwise, he may face an exhaustive and ultimately fruitless search. Another factor is whether the item can be found rapidly. Given these factors, it is possible that one conditioning technique may give better practical performance than another, theoretically superior, one.

6.2   Actual use of UNIX history

We have seen that user dialogs are highly repetitive and the last few command lines have a high chance of recurring – the premise behind most history systems. There are certainly plenty of opportunities for reuse, especially when appropriate conditioning methods are engineered into the presentation of items. But are current history mechanisms used well in practice? And how are they used? This was investigated by analyzing each user's *csh* history use. During data collection, all *csh* history uses were noted, although the actual form of use was not. Results should be interpreted carefully, for they may be artifacts arising from idiosyncrasies of the *csh* facilities, rather than from fundamental characteristics of reuse.

The recurrence rate and its probability distribution, studied previously, give a theoretical value against which to assess how effectively history mechanisms are used in practice. The average rate of reselecting items through a true sequential history list (as used by *csh*) cannot exceed the average value of $\mathcal{R}$, which was found to be 74%. By comparing the user's actual reselection rate with this maximum, the practical effectiveness of a particular history mechanism can be judged.

6.2.1   Results

Table 6.6 shows how many users of UNIX *csh* in each sample group actually used history. Although 54% of all users recalled at least one previous action, this figure is dominated by the computer sophisticates. Only 20% of Novice Programmers and 36% of Non-programmers used history, compared to 71% for Computer Scientists and 92% for Experienced Programmers.

Those who made use of history did so rarely. On average, 3.9% of command lines referred to an item through history, although there was great variation ($std\ dev = 3.8$; $range = 0.05\% - 17.5\%$). This average rate varied slightly across groups, as illustrated in Table 6.6, but an analysis of variance indicated that differences are not statistically significant ($F(3, 86) = 1.02$).

In practice, users did not normally refer very far back into history. With the exception of novices, an average of 79%–86% of all history uses referred to the last five command lines. Novice Programmers achieved this range within the last two submissions. Figure 6.3a illustrates the nearsighted view into the past. Each line is the running sum of the percentage of history use accounted for (the vertical axis) when matched against the distance back in the command line sequence (the horizontal axis). The differences between groups for the last few actions (left-hand side of the graph) reflect how far back each group prefers to see.[4]

Because most activities revolve around the last few submissions, the distribution bears closer examination. The data points in Figure 6.3b now represent the percentage of history use accounted for by each reference back. High variation between groups is evident. Although most uses of history recall the last or second-last entry, it is unclear which is referred to more.

It was also noticed that history was generally used to access or slightly modify the same small set of command lines repeatedly within a login session. If history was used to recall a command line, it was highly probable that subsequent history recalls will be to the same command.

A few *csh* users were queried about history use. They indicated that they are discouraged from using *csh* history by its difficult syntax and the fact that previous events are not normally kept on display. (The latter point is important, for it enforces the belief that candidates for reuse should be kept on a display.) Users also stated that most of their knowledge of UNIX history was initially learned from other people – the manual was incomprehensible. Also, the typing overhead necessary to specify all but the simplest retrievals makes users feel that it is not worth the bother.

6.2.2 *Corroboration and extensions*

Another researcher, Alison Lee, also examined history usage within various command interpreters available to the UNIX environment. Some of her qualitative findings corroborate and add to the observations noted in this section (Lee and

---

[4]Actual figures are probably higher than those indicated here, due to inaccuracies in distance estimates. As the *csh* monitor noted only that history was used and not how it was used, the actual event retrieved was determined by searching backward for the first event exactly matching the current submission. If the submission was a modified form of the actual recalled event, the search would terminate on the wrong entry. I assume that these are a small percent of the total.

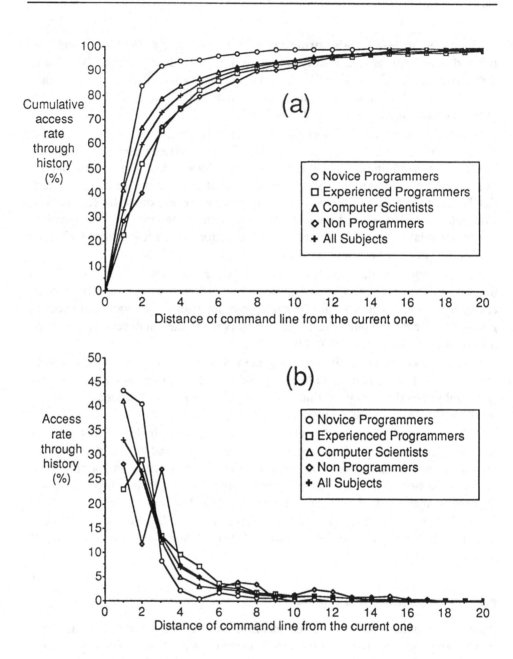

Figure 6.3. (a) Cumulative distribution of history; and (b) distribution of history use as a measure of distance.

Lochovsky, 1990).

1. There were very few uses of *csh* history.
2. Those uses made were of the simpler features, the most popular being "!!" (retrieve the last event) and "!pattern" (retrieve the most recent event beginning with the given pattern).
3. People rarely retrieved items by absolute or relative event number.
4. Although the history list is available for viewing by special request, users rarely asked to see it.
5. Modifiers for editing were rarely used. When used, they tended to be of the form $\wedge pattern1 \wedge pattern2\wedge$, which does simple sub-string replacement on the previous submission.
6. Other observed ways of modifying events were by using recalled events as prefixes or suffixes. This technique allows one to add more parameters to previous events or to add a new command sequence in a pipeline.
7. Occasional uses were noted of recalling the last word in the previous event (i.e., !$) and of printing events without executing them.

Lee also looked at *tcsh*, another history mechanism available to UNIX users that employs a very simple and familiar *emacs*-like editing paradigm to retrieve, review, and edit previous events. Although better use of history is expected because of the improved editing power and visualization of the history list, only a marginal increase was noted (although the still-available *csh* history was used less). The visual scrolling and editing capabilities available in *tcsh* were used to some extent.

6.2.3 Discussion

Many people never use UNIX *csh* history. Those who do tend to be sophisticated UNIX users. Yet even they do not use it much. On average, less than 4% of all submissions were retrieved through history out of the 74% potentially possible. The history facility supplied by *csh* is obviously poor.

Some reasons for the failure of *csh* history follow. First, the complex and arcane syntax discourages its use. Those who did use history indicated that only the simplest features of UNIX history were selected. As one subject noted, "it takes more time to think up the complex syntactic form than it does to simply retype the command." Also, it takes at least two or more characters to recall an event in *csh*. Because most simple UNIX recurrences are short (6 characters on average), users feel that it is not worth the bother. Second, it is hard to find out about it. *Csh* details are buried in a single on-line manual entry that runs to thirty-one pages(!), the text is quite technical, and examples are sparse. Third, the event list is usually invisible. Because previous events are not normally kept on the display, frailty of human memory usually limits recall to the last few items. These deficiencies of *csh* hit Novice Programmers especially hard. Even though they have the highest recurrence rate of all groups and could benefit the most from history, they are effectively excluded from using it.

It is too early to condemn the ideas provided by *csh*, because some of the observations are likely artifacts of using a poorly designed facility, rather than a human difficulty with the idea itself. Still, it is worthwhile to review some strong and weak points of the common history methods used.

Retrieval through absolute or relative position.   It is fairly difficult to associate and remember the number of a previous event, because it is an indirect reference. Visibly tagging events with numbers offers a benefit only for those interfaces without direct selection and only when no better strategy is available. Perhaps its sole viable use is as a redundant way of retrieving events when other selection methods are available.

Scrolling and hidden views.   If events are not on display, they will not be asked for. Hidden history lists were rarely recalled, and little use was made of the scrolling facilities in *tcsh*.

Pattern matching.   Simple pattern matching, especially by prefix specification, seems promising as a textual way of retrieving events. But matching is potentially dangerous, as users may accidentally retrieve and execute an interposed but undesired event that fits the specification.

Simple methods for recall/selection of very recent events.   The   syntactically simplest methods are used most to recall very recent events. For example, the "!!" directive was heavily used, even though it does not recall the most probable event. This probably reflects the shortness of short-term memory – users use only "!!" because the last item is the only thing they can both remember reliably and retrieve quickly.   Overloading a reuse facility with complex functionality would not make it better.

Editing events.   Although people do edit command lines as they compose them, they may not be willing to modify previous events much. Often the cognitive and physical overhead of recall and editing previous events makes simple reentry more effective. Still, some editing does occur and probably has some value.

6.3   Concluding remarks

The first part of this chapter explored further the potential opportunities for reuse in the UNIX *csh*. In particular, a variety of conditioning methods were described and evaluated. Each method used different strategies for choosing a small set of previous submissions as predictions of the next one. We saw that up to 55% of all user activity and 3.3 characters per submission can be predicted successfully with working sets of just ten predictions. The best any literal predictive method could do is $R = 75\%$ on average, or 4.4 characters per submission. Although conditioning methods are about 75% effective, there is still considerable room for improvement.

The number of characters saved per submission may seem quite small. The skeptic would conclude that reuse facilities are perhaps not worth the fuss. But a few points should be considered. First, the number of characters saved in practice would be considerably higher, for the string is already formed and editing is not necessary. Command line entry involves not only typing the final correct characters, but also the time it takes to detect and correct typing errors. Actual character savings are likely *double* the theoretical ones (Whiteside, Archer, Wixon, and Good, 1982). Second, recognizing and selecting an activity is generally considered easier than recalling or regenerating it. We expect a considerable time savings. Third, it may all depend upon the user's focus of attention. If he is selecting items from a history list with (say) a mouse, he may continue to do so rather than switch to the keyboard. The reverse is also true.

In marked contrast, the second part of this chapter discovered that *csh* history is used poorly in practice. Most people, particularly those who are not computer sophisticates, do not use it. Those who do, use it rarely. Only 4% of all activity was reused, compared to the 75% possible! And in spite of the esoteric features available in *csh* history, only the simpler features were used with any regularity. It was suggested that the results observed are likely artifacts of using a poorly designed facility, rather than a human difficulty with the idea of reuse.

7

Principles, corroboration, and justification

The two preceding chapters analyzed command line recurrences with dialogs with the UNIX *csh*. Based on the empirical results, the first section of this chapter formulates general principles that characterize how users repeat their activities on computers. Some guidelines are also tabulated for designing a reuse facility that allows users to take advantage of their previous transaction history. The second section corroborates these principles by a post hoc study of user traces obtained from another quite different command line system. The final section steps back from the empirical findings and presents a broader view of reuse.

7.1   Principles and guidelines

This section abstracts empirical principles governing how people repeat their activities from the UNIX study described earlier. They are summarized and reformulated in Table 7.1 as empirically based general guidelines for the design of reuse facilities. Although there is no guarantee that these guidelines generalize to all recurrent systems, they do provide a more principled design approach than uninformed intuition.

7.1.1   Principles: how users repeat their activities

A substantial portion of each user's previous activities are repeated. In spite of the large number of options and arguments that could qualify a command, command lines in UNIX *csh* are repeated surprisingly often by all classes of users. On average, three out of every four command lines entered by the user have already appeared previously. UNIX is classified as a recurrent system by the definition in Section 5.1.

This high degree of repetition justifies the intent of reuse facilities. Recurring inputs should be reentered more easily than the user's original entry, with the aim of reducing both physical tedium and the cognitive overhead of remembering past inputs. Reuse facilities should not be targeted only to experts, as they can help everyone.

New activities are composed regularly. Although many activities are repeated, a substantial proportion is new. One out of every four command lines entered to UNIX *csh* is a new submission. Composing command lines is an open-ended activity.

Table 7.1. *Design guidelines for reuse facilities*

Design guidelines
⊙ Users should be able to recall previous entries.
⊙ It should be cheaper, in terms of mechanical and cognitive activity, to recall items than to re-enter them.
⊙ Simple reselection of the previous five to ten submissions provides a reasonable working set of possibilities.
⊙ Conditioning of the history list, particularly by pruning duplicates and by further hierarchical structuring, could increase its effectiveness.
⊙ History is not effective for all possible recalls, because it lists only a few previous events. Alternative strategies must be supported.
⊙ Events already recalled through history by the user should be easily reselected.

Many modern interfaces provide transient menus as a way of structuring and packaging common activities. Though useful for appliance-oriented systems (Section 1.2.2), this package of favored submissions will not suffice as a front end to the general-purpose environments addressed in this book. Although the few facilities shared by users should be enhanced somehow, user composition of new command lines must be supported as well.

Users exhibit considerable temporal recency in activity reuse. The major contributions to the recurrence distribution are provided by the last few command lines entered.

As shown in Chapter 4, most reuse facilities are history mechanisms designed to facilitate reentry of the last few inputs. Systems that do not have explicit and separate displays of the event list rely on users remembering their own recent submissions, or on the visibility of the dialog transcript on the (usually small) screen. Given the high recency effect, we do expect limited success by memory alone. Yet the principle does pinpoint design weaknesses of existing systems.

First, the second-to-last command line recurs more often than any other single input. But many reuse facilities favor access to the last entry instead. For example, typing the shortcuts "redo" and "!!" in the *programmer's assistant* and UNIX *csh* respectively defaults to the previous submission, and it is slightly harder to retrieve other items. In history through editing, a user would have to search through two previous mixings of input and output before finding the second-to-last entry.

Second, the major contributions to the recurrence distribution are provided by the previous 7 ± 3 inputs. Yet most graphical history mechanisms display considerably more than ten events. HISTMENU, for example, defaults to fifty-one items, and *window management window* is illustrated with eighteen slots (Section 4.1.2). Considering the high cost of real estate on even large screens, and the user's cognitive overhead of scanning the possibilities, a lengthy list is unlikely to be worthwhile. For example, a menu of the previous ten UNIX events covers, on average, 45% of all inputs. Doubling this to twenty items increases the probability by only 5%.

The cost/benefit tradeoff of encompassing more distant submissions could also be used to tune other predictive systems that build more complex models of all inputs (Section 4.2). The high recency effect associated with recurrences suggests that a reasonable number of successful predictions can be formed on the basis of a short memory. Perhaps a recency-based short-term memory combined with a frequency-based long-term memory could generate better predictions.

Some user activities remain outside a small local working set of recent submissions. A significant number of recurrences are not covered by the last few items (about 40% of the recurring total with a working set of ten events). Doubling or even tripling the size of the set does not increase this coverage much, as all but the few recent items are, for practical purposes, equiprobable.

Unfortunately it is just these items that could help the user most. Because their previous invocation happened long ago, they are probably more difficult to remember and reconstruct than more recent activities. If the command line is complex, file names would be reviewed, details of command options looked up in a manual, and so on. Except for systems with pattern matching capabilities and scrolling – both questionable methods of recall – no implemented reuse facility provides reasonable ways of accessing distant events. Chapter 8 will explore a few alternative strategies.

Working sets can be improved by suitable conditioning. A perfect "history oracle" would always predict the next command line correctly, if it were a repeat of a previous one. Because no such oracle exists, we can only contemplate and evaluate methods that offer the user reasonable candidates for reselection. Although simply looking at the last few activities is reasonably effective – 60% of all recurrences are covered by the previous ten activities – pruning duplicates, context sensitivity, partial matches, and hierarchies of command-sensitive sub-lists all increase coverage to some degree. Combining these methods is also fruitful. But they have drawbacks too.

Pruning duplicates increases the coverage of a fixed-size list. However, if sequences of several events can be selected (as in the *programmer's assistant*, Section 4.1.1), pruning may destroy useful sequences. And events no longer follow the true execution order, confounding attempts to recall them by position. Pruning problems also arise when the history list serves other purposes. Consider, for example, the undo facility in the *programmer's assistant*. Because side effects of activities are stored along with the text of the activity, undoing two textually equivalent items may have different results. In this case, items cannot be pruned without compromising the integrity of the undo operation (Thimbleby, 1990).

Conditioning the working set on the current working directory may eliminate useful context-independent items from the history list with only a slight gain in predictive power. But the usefulness of references may improve, because viewing the history list may help remind the user of the specialized and perhaps more complex directives submitted in that context.

Retrieval by partial matching allows a user to select any event and edit it for spelling corrections or minor changes. There is no guarantee that the editing overhead will be less than simple reentry. The possibility of erroneously retrieving an undesired event must be considered too.

When command-sensitive sub-lists are included but ignored, the potential for reuse is still at least as high as the primary list. Using the attached sub-lists can only increase the chance of finding a correct match. Still, these sub-lists involve considerably more mechanical overhead for reuse unless they are on permanent display, and even then there is a cognitive overhead.

Some seemingly obvious or previously implemented ways of presenting predictions do poorly. Scrolling through alphabetically sorted submissions is ill-suited to activity reuse. Yet this scheme pervades many modern, popular systems. The Apple Macintosh, for example, presents a scrollable alphabetic display of files for selection within its applications. If file use is a recurrent system (which it probably is), then structuring file lists by temporal recency could give quicker selection, especially with large file stores.

The previous chapter has shown that saving duplicates in their original position is an extremely poor predictive strategy for maintaining lists. Yet it is used by several history systems. It is the only method of reviewing cards visited in HY-PERCARD, and it is a presentation option in *window management window* (Section 4.1). Different strategies should be encouraged.

Ordering lists by frequency of use may or may not give any benefit over recency. Although used fruitfully by the ADAPTIVE MENUS system (Greenberg and Witten, 1985a), the usability and predictive power of that system could perhaps increase if recent selections were treated preferentially, perhaps by giving them their own display space on the top-level menu screen.

Predicting commands without their arguments has little value. Although predictability is increased, the overall quality of prediction drops because mostly short sequences are offered. Perhaps inclusion of command-sensitive sub-lists could improve this fault.

When using history, users continually recall the same activities. UNIX *csh* users generally employ history for recalling the same events within a login session. Once an event has been recalled, it should somehow be given precedence.

Functionally powerful history mechanisms in glass teletypes do poorly. UNIX *csh* history fails on two points, even though it is functionally powerful. First, most people (especially novices and non-programmers) never use it. Second, those who do, use it seldom. Only a fraction of all recurrences are recalled through history.

7.2 Corroboration

The general principles of the previous section are based on the UNIX findings. There is no guarantee that they generalize to all recurrent systems and applications. It is useful to see if studies of other systems would produce the same results.

Data on a functional programming language called GLIDE was made available to the researcher after completion of the UNIX study. Because the principles of the previous section had already been elucidated, the GLIDE analysis is a post hoc study. The first part of the section briefly introduces GLIDE and describes the data collection method and the subjects. The second part lists the analysis performed and gives the results.

7.2.1   The GLIDE study

A brief description of GLIDE. GLIDE is an exploratory functional programming environment, supporting a lazy functional language, also called GLIDE (Toyn and Runciman, 1988). GLIDE programs consist of a collection of definitions and an expression to be evaluated. Definitions are partitioned into sets called flocks. GLIDE is built upon UNIX and exploits the UNIX file system, with definitions being files, and flocks being directories. UNIX commands are accessible from the GLIDE environment by using the *Shell* command or '!', which is consistent with other UNIX-based tools. Although definitions can be composed directly in the GLIDE environment, they are usually created, maintained, and imported through a standard UNIX editor. The command set in GLIDE is relatively small: twenty-three commands in total at the time of data collection (Finlay, 1988).

Table 7.2 gives a mythical and self-explanatory extract of an example GLIDE transcript. GLIDE prompts are boldface, and comments are distinguished by italics.

Subjects and subject use. GLIDE is used to teach functional programming to computer science undergraduates at the University of York (U.K.), and is also used by staff and graduate students in the course of their research. GLIDE usage by eighty such real users was logged unobtrusively over a three-month period for the purpose of studying the nature of expertise (Finlay, 1988). For the present study, twenty students and staff members having large logs were selected from the eighty participants.

Table 7.2. *A simple GLIDE dialog*

glide> Edit member	*The function definition (not shown) is created and edited in a UNIX file called member.g. Member checks if an element (its first argument) is contained in a list (its second argument). The appropriate boolean value is returned.*
glide> Define t1 ← [1.2.3.5.6]	*A definition called t1 comprising a list is created.*
glide> !cat member.g	*The user reviews the definition of member.*
glide> member 8 t1	*Is 8 a member of t1?*
False	
glide> member 2 t1	*Is 2 a member of t1?*
True	

Data collection. The original data consisted of the complete transcripts of GLIDE sessions, including commands issued by the user, the system's response, the function definitions imported from the editors, and a time stamp of the activity (second method, Section 2.2.1). The data was reduced for our analysis by stripping all information except for user input lines. These lines were further manipulated by removing the ones containing obvious errors, in particular misspellings of commands, incorrect recall of definitions, and syntactical misuse of commands. The final form of a single subject's data is a data file containing the subject's input lines in time-sequence order. The average data file contained 615 input lines, although there is much variation (*std dev* = 492.2).

Analysis. The analysis was similar to the UNIX one described in Chapters 5 and 6, although not nearly as extensive. The recurrence rate $\mathcal{R}$ is found and the probability distributions of recurrences for several conditioning techniques are detailed. These techniques are sequential ordering by recency with duplicates in place and duplicates pruned, frequency ordering, and a hierarchy of command lines with command-sensitive sub-lists. The metrics $\mathcal{R}_d$, $\mathcal{R}_D$, M_d, and M_D are calculated over each distribution.

7.2.2 Results and discussion

The average recurrence rate $\mathcal{R}$ is 50.2% with a standard deviation of 11.1%. Extremes range from 34% to 71.1%. The average length of a GLIDE input line is 12.6 characters, where terminating line feeds are not counted and duplicate lines are included. The average length of submissions that already exist on the history list is 9.7 characters, whereas those that appear for the first time are 15.5 characters long. Therefore maximum possible value for M_D is $\mathcal{R} \times 9.7/100$, which is 4.87

characters.

Table 7.3 summarizes the results for selected conditioning methods, where each row presents the values of the various metrics over the last fifty items on the history list. Figure 7.1 graphs the metric $\mathcal{R}_D$ on the vertical axis; the horizontal axis shows the position of the repeated GLIDE command line on the history list relative to the current one. Figure 7.2 is similar, except that the vertical axis now represents M_D (cf. Figures 6.1 and 6.2).

The results are quite similar to the results found in the UNIX study. The most glaring difference is the lower recurrence rate (50% vs. 75%). Part of this difference could arise from the fact that arguments in GLIDE functions are lists. Because lists are generally not as persistent as file names, arguments (and their lines) would not recur as often. Another part of this difference could be an artifact in data collection, for white space and errors are handled differently. First, although all unimportant white space was removed by *csh* in the UNIX study, this was not done for GLIDE. Recurrences arising from two semantically identical lines with syntactically different white spaces are not counted as a repeating submission. Second, errors in the UNIX study were marked when a *csh* error message was produced. GLIDE had no such capability, and most semantic errors were not tagged, although quite a few syntactic ones were removed manually. Because errors are generally not repeated, the number of unique lines is overestimated. Still, these artifacts are not expected to change the value of $\mathcal{R}$ greatly.[1]

When conditioning methods are contrasted for GLIDE, they follow the same rank ordering as that produced by *csh* use. Although there are fewer recurrences with GLIDE, the predictive power of the conditioning methods is relatively greater. For example, up to 43% of all user activity can be successfully predicted with working sets of ten predictions. Given that $\mathcal{R} = 50\%$, which is the best a perfect reuse facility could do, the best predictive method is 85% effective for GLIDE recurrences (cf. 75% for UNIX). When the quality metric is incorporated, up to 4.43 characters are saved per submission when ten predictions are available. Because the maximum value of M_D is 4.87 characters, the best method is about 90% effective (cf. 75% for UNIX).

In summary, despite the numeric differences in the analyses, the principles developed from the UNIX study are corroborated by subjecting GLIDE to the same analysis. Although new activities are composed regularly by users (around 50%), a substantial portion of their activities are repeated (50%). Users exhibit considerable recency in activity reuse in the same way they do with UNIX. The major contributions are provided by the previous 7 ± 3 submissions, and the second-to-last command line recurs more often than any other input (Table 7.3). Although some user activities still remain outside a small working set containing the recent submis-

---

[1] The recurrence rate calculated over GLIDE logs including errors is 48.6%, just a few points lower than the logs with errors removed manually.

Table 7.3. *Evaluating various conditioning methods in GLIDE*

Conditioning method	Distance													
	1	2	3	4	5	6	7	8	9	10	20	30	40	50
Probabilities of a recurrence at the given distance d in percent (R_d)														
Recency, duplicates saved	5.74	13.00	6.25	4.12	2.55	1.71	1.30	1.10	0.83	0.68	0.33	0.13	0.10	0.09
Recency, duplicates pruned	5.74	13.41	7.15	4.40	2.77	1.77	1.54	1.14	1.03	0.74	0.25	0.18	0.04	0.03
Frequency order	7.28	4.30	3.1	2.95	2.45	2.08	1.76	1.71	1.61	1.36	0.52	0.44	0.21	0.13
Command hierarchy	5.74	15.69	8.34	4.87	2.85	1.80	1.35	1.19	0.87	0.61	0.23	0.17	0.03	0.01
Accumulated probabilities of a recurrence up to a given distance d in percent (R_D)														
Recency, duplicates saved	5.74	18.74	24.99	29.11	31.66	33.37	34.67	35.78	36.61	37.29	41.44	43.54	44.76	45.62
Recency, duplicates pruned	5.74	19.15	26.30	30.70	33.47	35.24	36.78	37.92	38.94	39.69	43.54	45.58	46.72	47.43
Frequency order	7.28	11.58	14.68	17.63	20.08	22.17	23.93	25.64	27.25	28.61	37.11	41.52	43.97	45.34
Command hierarchy	5.74	21.43	29.77	34.63	37.48	39.28	40.63	41.82	42.68	43.30	46.49	47.97	48.74	49.08
The average number of characters saved over all subjects per recurrence at a given distance ($\bar{c}_d$)														
Recency, duplicates saved	8.16	10.22	10.41	10.80	10.97	8.53	9.80	8.97	7.65	8.18	5.97	5.07	3.23	4.16
Recency, duplicates pruned	8.16	10.20	10.59	10.60	10.20	9.42	9.11	9.09	7.76	6.94	6.08	3.59	2.11	1.30
Frequency order	6.49	8.29	8.63	8.35	8.78	10.32	10.11	10.61	9.81	9.90	7.83	7.84	5.19	5.31
Command hierarchy	8.16	10.65	10.61	10.33	9.97	9.38	8.36	9.00	7.59	8.23	6.50	3.91	1.73	1.35
Cumulative average savings in characters of D predictions over all submissions (M_D)														
Recency, duplicates saved	0.47	1.88	2.53	2.98	3.26	3.42	3.55	3.66	3.74	3.81	4.17	4.38	4.48	4.55
Recency, duplicates pruned	0.47	1.92	2.69	3.16	3.44	3.62	3.78	3.89	3.98	4.03	4.38	4.55	4.64	4.70
Frequency order	0.47	0.84	1.11	1.37	1.59	1.81	1.99	2.18	2.36	2.50	3.46	3.97	4.23	4.39
Command hierarchy	0.47	2.18	3.07	3.57	3.86	4.03	4.15	4.27	4.34	4.40	4.67	4.78	4.84	4.86

Note: Recurrence rate R is 50.24%. Maximum value of M_D is 4.89 characters.

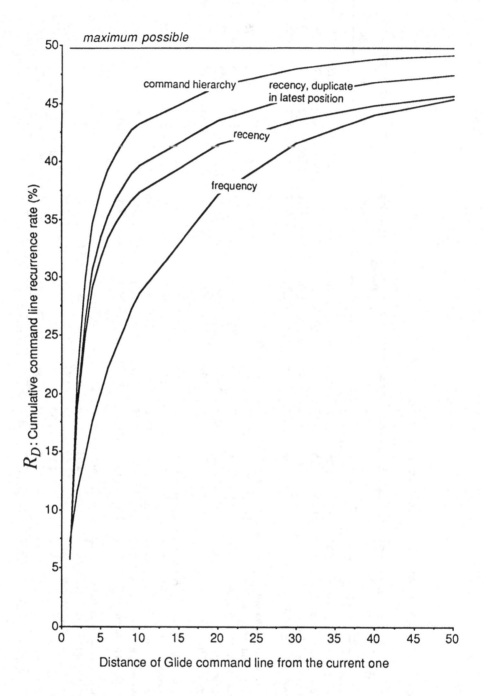

Figure 7.1. Cumulative probabilities of a recurrence over distance for various conditioning methods.

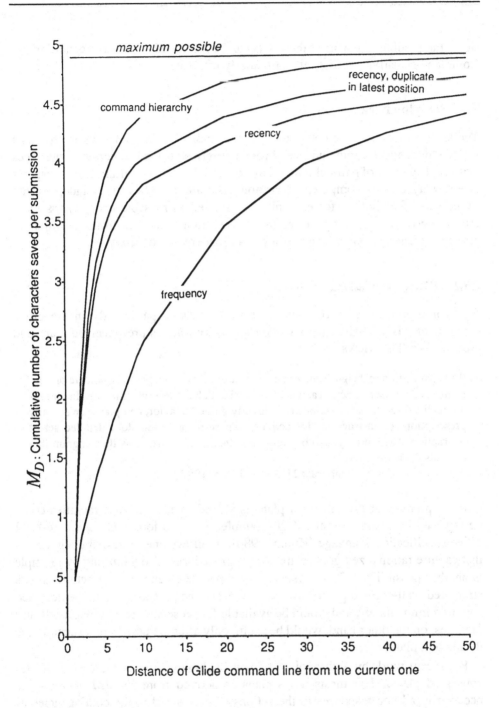

Figure 7.2. Cumulative average number of characters saved per submission over distance.

sions, the predictive power of these sets can be improved by suitable conditioning. Command-sensitive sub-lists are particularly effective.

7.3 Stepping back

The analysis made of the computer systems studied so far views an activity as a single independent command line. From a purely statistical standpoint, interfaces that simplify reuse of particular lines have potential to reduce certain tedious aspects of everyday human–computer interaction. But are activities really independent? Could sets of activities, for example, be grouped as reusable and perhaps more effective goal-specific scripts or plans? This section steps back from the empirical findings gleaned through observations to a broader view of reuse.

7.3.1 Plans and situated actions

A major design premise of some user support tools, particularly in the office environment, is the belief that a worker's activity follows preconceived plans and procedures.[2] This views

> the organization and significance of actions as derived from plans, which are prerequisite to and prescribe action at whatever level of detail one might imagine. Intentions are realized as plans-for-actions that directly guide behavior, and plans are actually prescriptions or instructions for actions. These plans reduce to a detailed set of instructions (which may also be sub-plans) that actually serve as the program that controls the action.
> — paraphrased from Suchman, 1987

If the premise of preconceived plans is indeed true, then reuse facilities could be replaced by planning tools. One example of such a tool is OSL, a high-level office specification language (Kunin, 1980). It allows one to describe algorithms that capture rationalized goal-related office procedures. Programming by example is another possibility. These systems allow people to encapsulate activities as a structured well-defined procedure (Section 4.3). The procedure could be designed and used immediately, and would be available for reuse any time thereafter. Reuse facilities, on the other hand, would be useful only after the user starts executing the details of a plan.

But recent work by anthropologist Lucy Suchman disputes the notion of preconceived plans. Her thesis treats plans as derived from *situated action* – the necessarily ad hoc responses to the actions of others and to the contingencies of particular situations.

---

[2]An argument parallel to the one in this section was developed independently by Lee and Lochovsky (1990).

> The course of action depends in essential ways upon the action's circumstances. Even casual observation of purposeful action indicates that, as common sense formulations of intent, plans are inherently vague as they are designed to accommodate the unforeseeable contingencies of actual situations of action. For situated action, the vagueness of plans is not a fault but, on the contrary, ideally suited to the fact that the detail of intent and action must be contingent on the circumstantial and interactional particulars of actual situations.
> — paraphrased from Suchman, 1987

Suchman suggests that: (1) plans are post hoc rationalizations of actions in situ; and (2) in the course of situated action, deliberation arises when otherwise transparent activity becomes in some way problematic.

But where does our belief in plans come from? According to Suchman, our descriptions of actions as purposeful always come before or after the fact, in the form of envisioned projections and recollected reconstructions.

> We can always perform a post hoc analysis of situated action that will make it appear to have followed a rational plan, for rationality anticipates action before the fact, and reconstructs it afterwards. Only after we encounter some state of affairs that we find to be desirable do we identify that state as the goal toward which our previous actions, in retrospect, were directed all along.
> — paraphrased from Suchman, 1987

Assuming that user activity on computers does follow situated actions, then reuse facilities are more viable than planning systems. Because reuse facilities allow one to select, possibly modify, and redo single actions, they respond well to the circumstances of a situation. When previous actions are collected as goal-related scripts of events, this flexibility is lost.

7.3.2 Recurrences: natural fact or artifact?

Where do recurrences come from? Are they a natural part of a human–computer dialog or are they artifacts imposed by poorly designed interfaces? If the former, then reuse facilities are an essential component of a good interface. If the latter, they are merely add-on patches; the interface itself should be reconsidered. We will see that, depending upon the situation, recurrences can be either.

The recency effect seen in recurrent systems is probably due to repetitive actions responding to interactional particulars of a situation that is changing only slightly. In a development task, for example, the situation may be debugging, where the usual responses to particular circumstances comprise a debug cycle. When the development is complete, the cycle terminates. Debug cycles are seen throughout the UNIX traces, and seem responsible for the recurrence probability peaking on the second-to-last submission. Consider this typical trace excerpt from a non-programmer developing a document.

```
nroff Heading2 Chapter1 | more
emacs Chapter 1
nroff Heading2 Chapter1 | more
emacs Chapter 1
nroff Heading2 Chapter1 | more
emacs Chapter 1
nroff Heading2 Chapter1 | more
emacs Chapter 1
nroff Heading2 Chapter1 | lpr –Plq &

. . .
```

The sequence shows the user developing a document by iteratively editing the source text and evaluating the formatted result on the screen, using the *emacs* editor and the *nroff* typesetter. The user's evaluation of the situation determines how often the cycle is repeated. When she was satisfied with the document, she terminated the cycle by producing a final hard copy.

Another extracted and slightly simplified sequence from a different user illustrates program development using the *fred* editor and the ada compiler.

```
fred
ada –M concur –o q5.o q5.a   | repeats 11 times


q5.o                         | repeats 3 times


fred
ada –M concur –o q5.o q5.a   | repeats 6 times
q5.o
```

This shows three debug cycles all related to the same development process. In the first, the user edits some source code until it successfully compiles (eleven cycles), and then evaluates the executable program. Final tuning of the program is done by expanding the initial debug cycle to include editing, compilation, and execution.

The actual development cycles seen support Suchman's thesis of situated actions. The user's plan for the development process is necessarily vague, because bugs and difficulties cannot be predicted beforehand. The developer must, of necessity, respond to the particulars of each individual situation. These responses appear repetitious because the situation is altered only slightly after each action.[3]

---

[3] Although repetitions in the UNIX dialog shown appear identical, the changes made within the editor application are not repetitious.

In the case of debug cycles, it is certain that some recurrences are artifacts that can be eliminated through different interfaces. Interpreted or incrementally compiled programming environments, for example, remove the necessity for repeated recompilation of the source (see Reiss, 1984 for an example). In other domains, what-you-see-is-what-you-get text processors and spreadsheets not only remove the "compile" step from the cycle, but also show the current state of execution. No distinction is made between the source and developing product, and any changes update the display immediately.

But other recurrences are not so easily eliminated. Repetitions are often a natural part of the task being pursued. Design work, for example, is fundamentally an iterative process. A second example is telephone dialing. The caller may dial the same number repeatedly when a connection is not made, or he may be a middleman arbitrating information between two or more other people. Retrieval of information in manuals is another example of recurrences that arise from repetition of our intentions rather than from interface artifacts. Or consider navigation on computers where people must locate and traverse the many structures necessary for their current context (e.g., navigating file hierarchies and menu-based command sets, and manipulating windows to find pertinent views). Because context switching is common, these traversals would recur regularly.

Other recurrences come from long-term context switching. In the UNIX traces, it is usual to see work on a particular task (say document development) occurring in bursts. In a single login session, these bursts may be just a single task interrupted by other dependent or independent diversions. Over multiple login sessions, tasks are constantly released and resumed.

In summary, some recurrences are artifacts arising from particular aspects of a system design and implementation. Others are not, for they arise directly from the user's intention, independent of the computer system. Perhaps future systems will minimize the need for reuse facilities by eliminating the artifacts. For the present, reuse facilities remain a potentially viable and very general way of handling repetition.

7.4 Concluding remarks

A set of empirically based principles of how people repeat their activities on computers was listed in this chapter. These principles were reformulated as general design guidelines for the design of reuse facilities. Although there is no guarantee that the principles apply to all recurrent systems and applications, they were supported by a post hoc analysis of usage transcripts of the GLIDE functional programming language. The chapter also discussed whether it is appropriate to treat activities as single, independent entities. It was argued that the course of action is a response to the current situation. As a consequence, single activities could more readily respond to changing situations than a preconceived plan. Finally, it was argued that recurrences are both natural facts arising from cognitive behavior and task requirements, and artifacts arising from poor interface design.

The appeal of a reuse facility is its potential benefit for any application dialog classified as a recurrent system. A reuse facility requires only that submissions entered to the application can be collected, presented, and selected for reuse. Because no semantic knowledge of the domain is needed, it is a general turnkey approach.

8

Organizing activities through workspaces

*In every trade a specific way of organizing tools and objects for the craftsman
has been established. Every workshop is equipped with appropriate tools and
organized with respect to the specific working situation. In this way strategies
for the solution of typical problems are at hand for the workers.*
—Hoffman and Valder, 1986

This book opened by advocating the common metaphor of tool use for thinking
about command-based systems, where command lines are the tools people employ
to manipulate the materials in their computer environment. The four preceding
chapters pursued the notion that recently used lines, like tools, should be available
for reuse. But reuse is not the only strategy for supporting user activities. It is
evident that people impose some organization on their computer tools and materials,
just as craftsmen do with their physical counterparts. Real workshops support these
organizations through toolboxes for arranging and locating tools, workbenches for
performing specific tasks, shelving and drawers for keeping relevant tools and
materials readily available, and so on. Computing environments, on the other
hand, do little to promote personal organization. A command-based interface is
comparable to an unhelpful clerk who waits for you to name the tool you want,
retrieves the tool (if available) from a separate room, and demands that you return
it immediately after use. At the other extreme, arranging facilities into fixed
taxonomic menus is reminiscent of a totalitarian chaining of tools to a single
location.

One theme of this research is that people mentally structure their activities
on computers, and that a software tool can be embedded into the interface to
support these implicit organizations. Section 8.1 reviews evidence that people's
activities are loosely related by tasks and by functionality, and can be grouped
accordingly. In particular, a user's normal computer interaction can be partitioned
into interleaved sets of goal-related tasks. The next section follows with several
relevant implications leading to design suggestions for a *workspace* – an interactive
software tool that collects and makes available a user's related materials in one
convenient location. Finally, a few existing implementations that profess to support
user organization are described to give the reader a feel for what is currently
available.

Table 8.1. *A user's task set for preparing a specific document*

Command line	Meaning
cd ~/Thesis	*go to the directory containing the desired file*
emacs Chapter1	*edit the file*
spell Chapter1 | more	*list the spelling mistakes in the file*
nroff Heading Chapter1 | more	*view the formatted file on the screen*
nroff Heading Chapter1 | lpr &	*produce a hard copy of the document on the standard printer*
nroff Heading Chapter1 | lpr –Pci &	*produce a hard copy of the document on the printer named "ci"*
rm *.BAK	*remove the backup files created by the editor*

8.1   Relating activities

Activities are not necessarily independent of each other, but may be related in many ways. In particular, users partition their actions and the objects they manipulate (such as files) into sets of goal-related tasks, called a *task set*. This was first articulated by Bannon, Cypher, Greenspan, and Monty (1983), who analyzed command line activity on a UNIX system by asking users to annotate their command histories periodically with their intentions. Their method and a short sample annotated trace were detailed previously in Section 2.2.2.

To illustrate the idea of a task set, consider the case of one non-programmer from the current study preparing a document (a thesis chapter). A review of her trace revealed that several command lines, listed in Table 8.1, were used consistently for this purpose. These lines did not always follow in the same order. The activity selected at any moment from the task set seemed to depend on the particular circumstances (see Section 7.3).

Tasks are not invoked sequentially, but are interleaved because the user switches, suspends, and resumes his goals. This is graphically illustrated by Cypher's analysis (1986) of the activity flow during one person's computer use for a single morning, reproduced in Figure 8.1. His analysis was based on the annotated history records collected by Bannon, Cypher, Greenspan, and Monty (1983). The boxes and sub-boxes in the figure represent the duration of the nineteen main activities observed and their further sub-activities. The user's progression through and between tasks is followed by the arrows, whereas activity performance is illustrated by the shaded areas. Annotations at the bottom describe the task. For example, the session starts with *read mail*, switches to *reposition window*, switches to *msg conversation*, and so on (Cypher, 1986). Each task shown may, of course, be made up of one or more activities.

Further evidence that users interleave task sets is provided by studies of window systems. Although all activity pertaining to a particular task is often confined to a single window, this is not necessarily the case. For example, the contents of

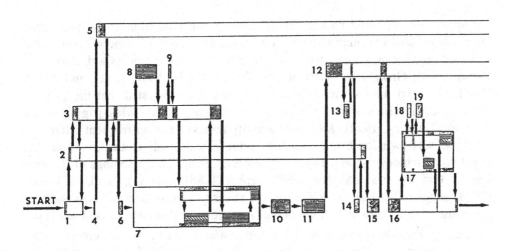

1	Read mail	8	Help A	14	Play with windows
2	Reposition window		Find note about "fmt"	15	Read new mail
3	Msg conversation		Try it out	16	Make a note
4	Check reminders	9	Delete outdated message	17	Save it as a good example
5	Arrange a meeting	10	Mail from Y		File it
	Check calendar		Find history programs		Find the sub-bin
6	Delete old messages	11	Fix the clock		Describe the example
7	Respond to P's message		Read documentation		Locate the text
	Send a reply		Ask for help	18	Retitle a note
	Set up a new account	12	Read over printouts	19	Make a main bin
	Log in to remote computer	13	Look at a note		

Figure 8.1. A user's flow of activities for one morning's computer use, from Figure 12.1 in Cypher, 1986.

multiple windows could be a different software representation of the same task. Or windows could be implicitly related by the information in one window being accessed (and perhaps combined with) the information in another (Card, Pavel, and Farrell, 1984; Greenberg, Peterson, and Witten, 1986). Card, Pavel, and Farrell (1984) recorded how a user selected windows and suggested that the patterns observed are reminiscent of the locality of reference behavior when paging virtual memory (Denning, 1970). Most user activity revolves around frequent references to a small set of windows, and a window "fault" often signals a transition to another small set of windows (Card, Pavel, and Farrell, 1984). These findings of Bannon, Cypher, Greenspan, and Monty (1983), Cypher (1986), and Card, Pavel, and Farrell (1984) suggest that task switching occurs at many levels: between sequences of input lines; between particular windows on a screen; and between sets of windows.

These studies do not show how task sets differ between users. Perhaps a clue can be gleaned from the work of Nielsen, Mack, Bergendorff, and Grischkowsky (1986), who investigated integrated software usage by professionals in a work environment. For each professional, they identified the main goals and sub-goals, as well as the methods used to satisfy the goals. Data was collected through questionnaires and interviews. Results were as follows.

- Five high-level application programs accounted for 42% of program use over the population.
- It was not possible to rank the programs accounting for the other 58% at the population level, as most were used by only a few professionals each.
- Integrated packages were not exploited fully. For example, users chose non-integrated modules if they were judged more effective in terms of goal achievement than the integrated version. In other words, users were "choosing a set of heterogeneous programs and integrating them in their own way."

Nielsen et al. conclude that integrated programs are not a panacea for communicating with general-purpose computers, for "most current analyses have not yet developed categories of representation adequate for identifying the task requirements of integration"(p. 167). Even so, the large number of different programs used by professionals and the different ways they were "integrated in their own way" suggests that there are both subtle and overt differences between the task sets of users.

Activities are also categorized according to the function they serve, rather than the particular task they address. By way of analogy, consider a mechanic's functionally arranged toolbox, where screwdrivers are located in one compartment, wrenches and sockets in a second, electrical equipment in a third, and so on. Although particular tools may be selected and placed on a workbench for a specific job (i.e., a task set of tools), the functional arrangement gives a good general organization. Functional organization is also possible in computers. For example,

Hanson, Kraut, and Farber (1984) classified UNIX commands into five general categories and measured their frequency of use.[1] The categories are generic editing commands that shape text and other objects (36%), orienting commands that inform users about their working environment (21%), process management commands used to integrate individual commands into more complex units (10%), and social commands that allow people to exchange information with each other (3%). The remaining 30% were task-specific commands. Individuals would, of course, have their own different classifications.

There are many other ways of organizing activities. Subactivities can be collected and treated as a single unit (e.g., pipelines, shell scripts). Activities may be categorized not by function but by the object they manipulate (e.g., file-centered). However, it is beyond the scope of this book to discuss further possibilities.

In summary, empirical evidence and intuitive insight suggest that activities are related in several ways. First, user activity is partitioned into multiple levels of interleaved task sets related by the user's own particular goals. Different users have different task sets. Second, activities can be associated either by function or by the object being manipulated. Third, sub-activities can be combined into a single chunk. It is self-evident that users organize their activities in many (perhaps vague) ways throughout the computer dialog. The only truly surprising thing is the lack of computer support for this kind of organizing activity.

8.2 Implications: suggestions for workspaces

Although people organize their activities on computers, many systems either do not make these organizations explicit, or do so in very restricted ways. Without on-line support, people must recall or reconstruct through memory the previously established set of activities, or they must use existing, perhaps inappropriate, groupings. And users cannot easily share groupings that could be mutually beneficial.

This book argues that the organization of activities should be made explicit and available for use through a software tool generically called a *workspace*. Through a workspace, users are able to collect, organize, and use their on-line materials, and switch between tasks. When combined with a reuse facility, users can not only select items that were recently entered, but could bring in activities recorded in the more distant past.

Although not new, the notion of a workspace is not as prevalent in the literature as might be expected. This section starts by surveying the few existing works of researchers who derived workspaces from empirical analyses. Suggestions for workspaces identified in these reports are reviewed. Additional suggestions

---

[1]Because the frequency of use was determined by population statistics, it is not clear how accurately they apply to the individual (Section 3.5).

believed to be important are described later.

8.2.1   A review of suggestions

The concept of a workspace has been proposed by other researchers, although the labels given to the work sometimes differ (e.g., workbenches, tool bins, tool instruments). Researchers seem to have their own reasons for recommending a strong explicit organization of user activities. The evidence is usually intuitive, rather than experimentally supported.

For example, Norman (1984a, 1984b) identifies four stages of user activity – intention, selection, execution, and evaluation – each requiring different interface support strategies. He suggests that "workbenches that collect together relevant files and software support in one convenient location" can enhance user activity in some of the stages noted above ((Norman, 1984b, p. 368). The visibility of these items provides information that aids both the formation of the intention and its selection. If items are arranged properly within the workbench, selected items can then be easily executed. Unfortunately, Norman does not elaborate further on his workbench idea.

Another example of a workspace recommendation comes from Nakatani and Rohrlich (1983), who describe a three-layer system of organizing collections of "soft machines" into a *tools* structure. A "soft machines" metaphor graphically realizes special-purpose machine-like interface for certain activities. They suggest that this scheme may fail if the collection of machines is somehow not organized.

> We want the collection organized so that we have easy access to all the machines needed for the project with no unneeded machines cluttering our work environment
> — Nakatani and Rohrlich, 1983, p. 23

They propose a method of integrating links between soft machines by using the analogy of tools in a workshop. The hierarchy used is a *tool bin* (which is the entire set of tools); a *workshop* (which collects similar tools); and a *workbench* (on which the actual work is done). Although they also suggest that this hierarchy should have a parallel *data* hierarchy, they do not elaborate any further.

The most comprehensive work to date is that of Bannon, Cypher, Greenspan, and Monty (1983). Building on their work describing interleaved task sets, they propose an environment that allows users to arrange activities so that their goals and sub-goals are easily achieved. They suggest several guidelines.

1.   Reduce a user's mental load when switching tasks.
2.   Support suspension and resumption of activities.
3.   Maintain records of activities.
4.   Allow functional groupings of activities.
5.   Provide multiple perspectives on the work environment.

6.   Allow interdependencies among items in different workspaces.

Because tasks are frequently suspended and resumed, users should be able to navigate easily between activities (points 1 and 2). This was further elaborated by Card and Henderson (1987), who add the following to the wish list.

7.   Task switching should be fast.
8.   Task resumption should be fast.
9.   It should be easy to reacquire one's mental task context.

Workspaces can act as visible placeholders to reduce one's mental load. They should save and restore the task state between excursions. Also, the amount of cognitive overhead when switching tasks should be reduced by allowing the user to jot down notes and attach them to particular workspaces.

Users may wish to repeat an action identical or similar to one invoked recently (point 3), a major argument of this book. Bannon, Cypher, Greenspan, and Monty (1983). Bannon, Cypher, Greenspan, and Monty (1983) suggest that reusable context-sensitive records of activity should be included within the workspace.

The obvious function of a workspace is to group activities (point 4). These relationships should be defined by the user, as we will discuss in the next section.

Workspaces are not necessarily independent of one another, and relationships between them should be supported (points 5 and 6). Multiple instances of particular items should be allowed, as items from one workspace can be useful in another. Information in one workspace may be important and/or related to another, and the display should make interrelations obvious. Items should be collectively shared among several tasks, and their presentation should be task-specific (Card and Henderson, 1987).

8.2.2   Additional workspace suggestions

The suggestions in the preceding section, though important, are confined to support for task switching. The following discussion supplements the list of design suggestions that should be fulfilled by workspaces. It emphasizes the role of symbols, end-user personalization, and building structures by collecting previous – instead of anticipated – activities.

Abstracting activities through symbols. Although primitive activities (such as UNIX command lines) must be recorded in a workspace if they are to be reused, they need not be presented to the user in their native form. Instead, syntactic computer actions can be abstracted as symbols known to the user, where these symbols remind users of the meaning behind the action.[2] The expected effect is to minimize the need to translate the users' desire into the syntactic actions of the system by providing them with their own meaningful language (Shneiderman and Mayer, 1979; Perlman, 1984).

When symbols are both visible and selectable, they can be much more useful than the conventional abbreviations provided by most command-based systems. For example, a symbol might be a mouse-sensitive item selected from a menu, panel, or iconic display. When selected, the underlying action is executed. There is no need for the user to have to recall the name of the symbol or the syntax of the action invoked.

Symbols are, of course, not new to computer systems. What is novel is how they can be used within a set of workspaces to bring together related activities. A collection of symbols may represent the activities that make up a task set or functional grouping. The collection may be further abstracted as a symbol, which can itself be included in other collections. The desired effect is to represent a task set as a collection, and to provide links from one task to another. This supports interdependencies between workspaces. The user either executes particular activities within one workspace or calls up related workspaces by selecting the appropriate symbol. Multiple instances of workspaces are supported as well, because links need not be exclusive.

Symbols can also represent other attributes associated with an activity. Each entry can be annotated with extra information such as help text or a property sheet. Depending on how one selects the symbol, the activity may be executed, the help text displayed, or a property sheet raised for further clarification.

End-user personalization. Who actually builds and maintains workspaces – the overall structure, the activities included, and the symbols chosen? From the population perspective, designers can create default workspaces that are adapted by users to pursue common task sets. Previous chapters, however, argued that little activity overlap exists between individuals, implying the need for some level of personalization. Ideally, when a need arises that is not addressed well by the predefined workspaces, each user may immediately: (a) add, modify, or delete any elements within a given workspace; (b) create new workspaces or destroy old ones; and (c) alter the way workspaces are linked together. This capability is called "end-user personalization."

End-user personalization should allow individuals, including non-programmers,

---

[2]I use the term "symbol" according to its dictionary meaning: "a thing generally regarded as typifying, representing, or recalling something" (*Oxford Dictionary of Current English*, 1984). Other researchers have different definitions. Perlman, for example, describes a symbol as a letter representing a name, which in turn represents a concept (Perlman, 1984). The symbols here are not necessarily simple letters, but may be any textual or graphical representation of an activity.

to easily choose and arrange the tools and materials in their workspace. This requirement is vital, for designers can rarely predict user activity. Personal groupings exist (Sections 3.3 and 8.1). Particular users have their own unique task sets, and no universal scheme can cater to individual idiosyncrasies. Furthermore, user needs, tasks, and preferences change over time, and so workbenches should be easily modifiable.

Using old activities to construct workspaces. Users will not take advantage of a personalized workspace facility if it involves a significant overhead. The interface must therefore minimize the mechanical overhead of managing workspaces. More important is the cognitive overhead of forming activities collected by a workspace. If users must anticipate what they are going to do, then the burden of collecting the appropriate materials into the workspace will be high. People may not know precisely what activities are required for their task (Section 7.3). Even when they do, the activity desired must be composed, debugged, and tested to make sure that it will perform correctly. A better method would have users collecting their previous activities.

It was argued in Chapters 4 through 7 that people repeat their activities, and that a reuse facility has an important role in the human–computer interface. By merging this facility with a personalized workspace, and by making old activities also available as workspace items, considerable power can be gained. Users would not only be able to redo old actions but they could use the history list as the primary source of tried and tested candidates for their collections. They could select, copy, and add them directly into their workspace. I believe this novel synthesis is a major contribution of this research, because the potential benefits are so important. First, workspace items do not have to be anticipated. Instead, users can perform their tasks as normal and decide at any time to assemble the relevant previous activities that make up the task sets. Second, because these items are directly available, they are recalled rather than composed. Third, they have already been debugged and tested to some extent. Finally, interaction tedium is minimized, because modern techniques used for selecting and transferring activities (the cut/copy/paste metaphor) should take no more than a few seconds of time.

In summary, a workspace should allow a user to collect and abstract through symbols both new and previously entered activities into meaningful collections.

8.3 Implementations

Organizational strategies are not new to computer systems. Many top-level interfaces, for example, provide hierarchical directories for arranging files. Directories in common are prearranged by the system designer. Individual needs are also recognized – users may arrange their particular sub-tree of the hierarchy in any way they please.

Similarly, certain interfaces allow related actions to be grouped explicitly. Dedicated function keys are often arranged in clusters (e.g., cursor movement and editing actions). Attributes of objects may be listed and manipulated within property sheets (Witten and Greenberg, 1985). Hierarchical menus provide a hard-wired grouping of actions, where each menu page is dedicated to some predefined task (e.g., file manipulation). Products designed to address particular needs bundle selected activities into a single package.

Implementations related to workspaces fall into three broad categories: menu-based taxonomies, object-oriented browsers, and multiple virtual workspaces. Menus group activities – actions and perhaps their manipulated objects – into taxonomic chunks. Browsers, on the other hand, provide a rich development environment that is strongly tied to the explicit structure inherent in objects produced by object-oriented programs. Multiple virtual workspaces allow users to collect and navigate between screenfuls of windows. These three categories are described in greater detail in the following sub-sections, and are illustrated with a few implementations. Table 8.2 summarizes how six contemporary workspace designs fit the suggestions mentioned in the previous section. The list includes WORKBENCH, a design described in the next chapter. The intent is not to survey all workspace possibilities, but to give the reader a feel for how some important characteristics have been implemented.

Structuring activities through menus. Taxonomic menus classify a domain hierarchically and allow the user to navigate through it. In the process, the user attempts to focus on the desired information by refining the category that is currently displayed. These menus are familiar to computer users, and have been used to access information in very large databases (e.g., Videotex systems, Godfrey and Chang, 1981), and to organize activities in office automation systems (e.g., IBM AOSS).

A command interface to an operating system can be built using the same kind of taxonomic structure. For example, MENUNIX shows how an extensive and flexible operating system interface can be implemented with menus (Perlman, 1984). It allows access to the UNIX system by displaying two menus from which users can make selections: the *file menu*, which lists the current working directory, and the *program menu*, which lists the programs currently available (Figure 8.2). Command lines composed through these menus can be modified further using a line editor at the bottom of the screen, whereas previous submissions can be reselected through a small but visible history list.

When a file menu entry is selected, MENUNIX tries to do something sensible with the file. If it is a directory file, the current working directory will be changed. If it is an executable file, it will be run (after arguments are requested). If it is a text file, the user's preferred editor will be called on it. Thus users are able to edit files and change directories with just the file menu commands.

Table 8.2. *Suggestions implemented by existing workspace designs*

Property	MENUNIX	SMALLTALK	ROOMS	ROOM	WCS
			Task switching		
Reduces mental loads when switching tasks	Grouped activities saved in menus	All information retained between tasks	Window-based applications & window attributes saved between tasks	Task activities are saved as icons	Task activities are saved as pop-up menu items
Suspend and resume activities	No	Very slowly through projects	Rapid task switching through doors and Overview screen	Task switching through doors	Each workbench represented in its own window
Multiple perspectives of the work environment	No	Not really. Each project is independent of the other	Window collections are shareable between workspaces	Not known	Multiple instantiations of the same workbench are possible
Interdependencies among items	Menu items need not be unique between workbenches	Objects related through hierarchy	A window-based application can appear in any room	Copies of activity icons can be made and used in other rooms	Workbench links and menu items can be shared
			Grouping activities		
Functional groupings of activities	Yes, as items in a menu	Yes, as methods in an object and objects in a hierarchy	Yes, as collections of window-based application programs in a room	Yes, as activity icons in a room	Yes, as items in several pop-up menus attached to a workbench
End-user personalization of functions	Not expected	Only through programming	Window attributes and their applications are user defined	Icons are acquired through a "supply room" and their attributes can be altered.	All pop-up menu attributes are user defined

continued on next page . . .

. . . continued from previous page

Property	MENUNIX	SMALLTALK	ROOMS	ROOM	WCS
Reuse					
Maintain records of activities	Yes	No	No	No	No
Old activities transferable to workspace groupings	No	No	No	No	No
Symbols					
Abstracting activities with symbols	Yes, through descriptions and one-letter symbols	Yes, through class and message categories, objects, and message selectors	Limited. Doors represent rooms	Icons represent activities and doors represent rooms	Yes, with names, pop-up menu groups, and help messages
End user personalization of symbols	No	Through programming only	Rooms and doors can be named	Room maker allows rooms to be defined	Names, activities, and help messages are user defined

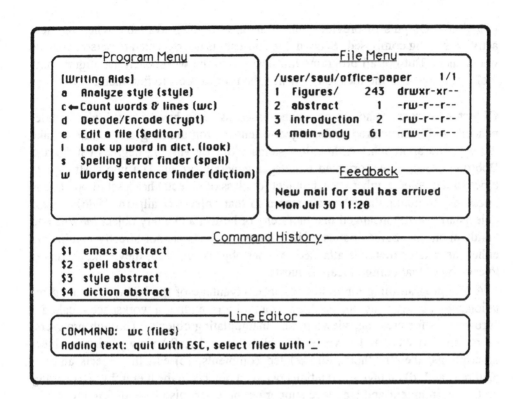

Figure 8.2. A stylized MENUNIX screen.

Programs are structured into "workbenches," and the program menu displays names (brief descriptions) of the programs in the current workbench. For example, one programming workbench contains sub-workbenches for general programming and specific programming languages. Other workbenches gather writing tools, deal with mail, and so on. When a program menu entry is selected, arguments are requested and the program is executed. To implement the hierarchy, an entry in a workbench may point to another workbench (in the same way that an entry in a directory may point to another directory in the file hierarchy). Selecting one of these entries will replace the current program menu accordingly. Of course, one consequence of having a program menu is that the vast selection of UNIX utilities must be structured somehow into reasonably small subsets fitting into each workbench; otherwise the menu would become unmanageable. In MENUNIX, this is the responsibility of the system administrator.

MENUNIX fulfills one of the workspace suggestions by using the workbench metaphor to gather groups of activities. Yet it fails as a workspace for two reasons (Table 8.2). First, it does not support most task switching activities. Only one workbench is visible at a time, and traversing the hierarchical links between them is tedious. Outputs of previous selections are not even available when the next activity is being composed. Second, the end-user is not expected to personalize the workbench. But not all programs fall neatly into the workbench paradigm; some tools may not be in the location in which the user expects to find them.

Object browsers. Whereas command-based systems have a multitude of independent and unstructured tools, object-oriented programming environments take the opposite approach. Although systems differ by varying degrees (Stefik and Bobrow, 1986), object-oriented languages generally group data into abstract data types called *objects*, where "each object (or class of objects) has a set of operations (*methods*) to manipulate the data stored in that object" (Hailpern, 1986). These objects are usually arranged in a hierarchy or lattice, and every object *inherits* and builds upon the characteristics of its parents. Objects cannot directly manipulate either the data or methods attached to other objects. Instead, they send *messages* to each other that communicate requests.

A few programming environments take advantage of the highly structured relationships between the objects they contain by providing a workspace – called a "browser" – for creating, viewing, and manipulating objects. Through browsers, users can: (a) view and traverse the object hierarchy; (b) view particular object descriptions, their methods, and related comments; (c) edit the objects and the methods; and (d) change the relations between objects in the hierarchy. Depending on the environment and language supported, browsers also have different capabilities. The SMALLTALK browser, for example, differentiates between the object's class and instance methods (Goldberg, 1984). LOOPS, on the other hand, supports multiple inheritance (Bobrow and Stefik, 1983), and the programmer can add, delete, rename, and split classes, and reorganize the lattice through the browser in a way that is not allowed in SMALLTALK (Stefik and Bobrow, 1986).

Figure 8.3 shows an example of the SMALLTALK browser in action. As shown, the browser is made up of five sub-views. The top four are menus that display, from left to right, class categories, classes, method categories, and message selectors. The large bottom sub-view is used mainly for editing templates of methods and class descriptions, although information about the object world is also displayed there (Goldberg, 1984).

What makes browsers particularly effective is the rigid classification of objects and actions within the environment. Unlike traditional systems (such as UNIX), each object understands only a limited set of actions. Similarly, action selectors (messages) are understood only by a restricted set of objects. A browser allows the programmer to inspect and use existing sets easily. When programming, objects and methods are easily added, deleted, and modified. Owing to the interdependencies between objects, it is vital for the programmer to view their relationships, for the programmer must know how to extend existing objects, and know which ones will be affected by any major changes.

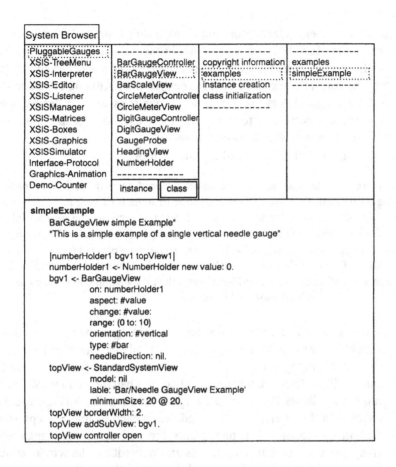

Figure 8.3. The SMALLTALK browser window.

Although object browsers are elegant workspaces for programmers, it is not clear whether this type of organization is reasonable for non-programmers. The browser's organizational strengths come from revealing the underlying structure of the object-oriented language, a structure that may be beyond the grasp and interest of a non-programming end-user. A further detraction is that although objects are extremely good representations of tightly related structures, they may be ill-suited for capturing the loosely related activities contained in task sets (Table 8.2).

Multiple virtual workspaces. Window-based systems allow users to manage a set of windows on a screen, where each screen is considered a single virtual workspace. A multiple virtual workspace is produced when the system remembers different screenfuls of window sets and allows transitions between them.

Perhaps the most exciting implementation to date that represents this concept is ROOMS, which divides groups of window-based applications into collections with transitions among them (Henderson and Card, 1986; Card and Henderson, 1987) Each screenful in ROOMS is a virtual workspace containing windows running specific applications. Many virtual workspaces exist, and a user can switch tasks by supplanting the current workspace with the desired one. Although designed mainly to reduce "thrashing" effects that occur when one tries to keep desired windows visible on a small screen, it effectively allows a user to organize collections of applications and move rapidly between them.

ROOMS brings together tasks and high-level tools.

> When there is some task to be done, such as reading mail, writing a paper, or creating a program, the user gathers a number of tools for doing it. ... The design of the ROOMS system is based on the notion that, by giving the user an interface mechanism for letting the system know he or she is switching tasks, it can anticipate the set of tools/windows the user will reference and thus preload them together in a tiny fraction of the time the user would have required ... the set of windows preloaded on the screen will cue the user and help reestablish the mental context for the task.
> — Henderson and Card, 1986

A single room looks like a standard screen containing a few special icons called "doors," which link the current room directly with others. Opening a door follows the metaphor of changing rooms. Every room also has a back door leading to the last room visited. One special room called an *Overview* shows all the rooms as pictograms and allows the user to navigate between them (Figure 8.4). Six rooms are shown in the figure, and the windows in each pictogram represent their actual layout in the room. The pictograms are active, as users may alter the internal arrangement of miniaturized rooms and redistribute the windows between the rooms through direct manipulation and the use of the delete, copy, move, and edit buttons. The last room visited is shown by its shaded label (the "Filing" room). Some additional points worthy of note are: windows can be shared between rooms, a window's presentation and position are linked to the workspace, rooms can be included in other rooms, windows can be carried from one room to another, and users can find out what rooms connect.

Henderson and Card (1986) mention that these multiple virtual workspaces are not new ideas. SMALLTALK, for example, has hierarchically arranged "projects" that define various working environments, each considered a virtual workspace (Goldberg, 1984). The CEDAR programming environment supports multiple "desktops" and allows users to choose between them through a desktop overview. And another UNIX-based system called *room* is a simpler version of the ROOMS metaphor above (Chan, 1984). Here, icons are collected into workspaces, and each icon either invokes a UNIX process (including parameters) or leads to another room. A special icon called a "room maker" lets a user specify new icons. The WORKBENCH CREATION SYSTEM is yet another virtual workspace offering that preceded ROOMS (Greenberg and Witten, 1985b). This experimental

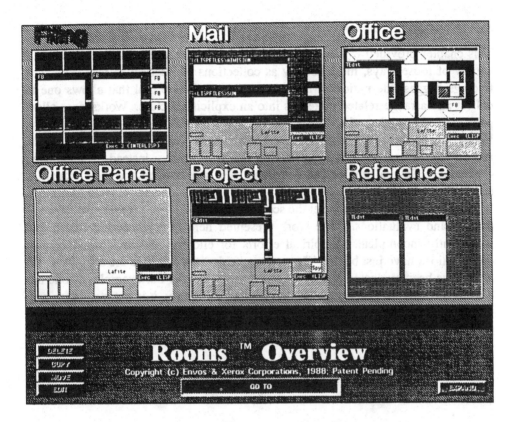

Figure 8.4. The ROOMS overview screen

interface used windows to provide multiple independent views into workbenches that collected a user's activities. What was novel about the WORKBENCH CREATION SYSTEM was that activities executed through pop-up menus and attached to the workbenches were user defined and maintained through a specialized direct-manipulation editor. All important aspects of this system are contained in the design and implementation detailed in the next chapter. A system somewhat similar to the WORKBENCH CREATION SYSTEM was developed later by Dzida, Hoffmann, and Valder (1987).

ROOMS allows users to bundle together windows running high-level applications (i.e., appliances, Section 1.2.2) with high-level tasks. But as seen in UNIX, much activity is generated at a low level, in that old lines are reused and new ones are formed continuously. Because there is no way to save a set of equivalent low-level activities in ROOMS, its value in a general-purpose environment is probably not as high as it could be. Informally speaking, ROOMS organizes workbenches within workspaces, but not the tools contained by each workbench (Table 8.2). Chan's *room* system, on the other hand, does provide this capability, albeit at a primitive and perhaps tedious level (Chan, 1984) (Table 8.2).

8.4 Concluding remarks

This chapter provided evidence that computer users organize their activities in a variety of loose ways, most notably as collections of interleaved task sets. The findings suggest the notion of a workspace – a software tool that allows one to collect and arrange related materials into an explicit structure. Workspaces allow personalized grouping of activities and rapid task switching between these groups. Furthermore, activities and their related attributes can be represented by symbols, and structures can be built by collecting one's previous – instead of anticipated – activities. Several implemented designs were summarized and their properties contrasted in Table 8.2.

This chapter is intended to set the scene for future studies, experiments, creative design, and evaluations. The work presented here is a pioneering effort, and is currently incomplete. Empirical efforts for eliciting and understanding user organizations have just begun. The notions behind a workspace are also weak, for none have been evaluated and tested to any great extent. For example, no one has directly investigated user-composed symbols.[3] Similarly, it is not clear how well users can articulate their task sets. What seems reasonable in theory may fail in practice.

---

[3]The closest study is one by Good, Whiteside, and Jones (1984), who suggest that user-derived commands improve a novice's ability to interact with a command system.

9

A workspace system: description and issues

*Basically, this workbench is composed of a pair of storage cabinets, on which
rests a rugged work top. The exact design of the storage cabinets depends on
the kind of work you do, the kind of tools you use, the amount of space you
have.*

—*Homeowner's How-to Treasury, Popular Science, 1976*

This chapter describes a design and implementation of a user support tool that
embodies the reuse properties suggested in Chapters 4 through 7, and the workspace
organization of Chapter 8.[1] Called WORKBENCH, the system is a graphical
window-based front end to UNIX *csh*. The facilities and user interface are described
in the first section, along with the rationale behind its design. WORKBENCH is
not an end in itself. Although recently made available to selected members of the
University of Calgary's Department of Computer Science and now used by several
people, it serves here as an exploration of a workspace design. It is not formally
evaluated; experimental appraisal is neither credible nor necessary at this early
stage. Rather, the intent is to discover how feasible it is to build a workspace, to
note initial pragmatic considerations arising from its use, and to suggest research
areas motivated by problems encountered or envisaged. These issues are covered
in the second section.

9.1   The WORKBENCH system

WORKBENCH is a window-based facility that allows people to reuse and structure
their on-line UNIX *csh* activities. It runs within the Sunview 4.0 window environment, and uses only the standard and familiar user interface constructs provided,
such as panels, buttons, pop-up menus, and so on (Sun, 1988). For consistency with
other Sunview applications, no attempt was made to change the "look and feel"
of these constructs. Although it caused a few problems, following this standard
nicely separated secondary interface design issues of window-based applications
from primary aspects of a workspace.

The first sub-section below gives a brief account of the several standard Sunview interface constructs used. The subsequent sub-sections provide an overview
of WORKBENCH, describe in detail its activity reuse facility, its organizational

---

[1] Some of the ideas in this chapter were presented at the Canadian Information Processing Society (CIPS)
National Conference in Montreal (Greenberg and Witten, 1985a).

capabilities, and finally its underlying architecture.

9.1.1 A brief overview of Sunview

Sunview is a user-interface toolkit that supports creation of interactive text and graphics-based applications running within a window environment available on SUN workstations. Although the building blocks supplied are moderately flexible, their usage in the WORKBENCH design is restricted to follow the standard user interface conventions pursued by most other Sunview applications. The look and feel of a few of the Sunview facilities selected are described here – frames, sub-windows, ttys, panels and their items, alerts, and menus. Programming details are omitted; they are amply covered elsewhere (Sun, 1988). A passing familiarity with window systems is assumed.

A *frame* acts as a window does in most window-based systems. It can be resized, moved around the screen, shrunk to an icon representation, selected for input, and so on. A frame is a Sunview object that brings together one or more other objects – frames or sub-windows – into a common framework so that they can be operated on as a unit. It can own non-overlapping *sub-windows* that are constrained to fit within the frame's borders, and other *sub-frames* that are often used to implement pop-up windows. Within a Sunview screen, a user will typically have several opened and closed windows on display (closed forms are represented by icons). Only one window at a time, chosen by moving the cursor into it, can receive textual input.[2]

Four types of sub-windows are available: canvas, text, panel, and tty. Programs can draw on a *canvas*, and text is presented and edited within *text* sub-windows. The *tty* is a terminal emulator, and only one is allowed per frame. *Panels* are sub-windows that contain a set of controls, called *panel items*. Although sub-windows do not overlap, they can be moved about in the frame under program or user control.

Menus are pop-up lists that display several choices for exclusive selection. Although menus can present non-executable information, a selection usually performs some system action. By convention, menus appear only when a user depresses the right mouse key, and disappear on the mouse key's release. Pointing to a menu item highlights it, whereas releasing the mouse key on the highlighted choice selects it. Special *pullright* menu items, distinguished by an arrow on their right, can display further menus. These sub-menus appear when the user moves the cursor rightward on the item.

Although there are many types of panel items, only the few used in the design are described here – buttons, cycle choices, and text items. *Buttons* are items that usually display a framed text string or a graphical image, and are selected by depressing the left mouse key and pointing to it, which inverts its color. An action is

---

[2] Alternatively, Sunview windows can be configured to accept the input focus by clicking a mouse key within it.

triggered when the mouse key is released. Moving the cursor off a button deselects it. Menus may be attached to buttons, and they appear when the right mouse key is depressed. Next, a *cycle choice* item allows the user to cycle through choices in a list. A descriptive text string is displayed on the left, the current choice on the right, and two semicircular arrows in between. A left mouse key click will cycle through the available choices one at a time, whereas depressing the right mouse key raises a menu of possible choices. Finally, *text items* display a label followed by an editable string field. Pointing to the field highlights the text and moves a text cursor into it. Editing capabilities are primitive: the cursor can appear just at the end of the string, and only backspace, word erase, and line erase are supported. When more characters are entered than will fit in the field, the displayed string is scrolled to the left. The presence of hidden characters is indicated by a left-pointing arrow.

Alerts are pop-up sub-frames that display a message and a set of buttons in a panel. As indicated by their name, they alert the user to some event. Unlike other sub-frames, the alert takes control of the entire screen until the user responds to it. These frames are distinguished visually from other windows by a large arrow that sweeps into them.

The Sunview window system, although popular, is by no means perfect. It is painfully slow on low-end workstations (e.g., the SUN 3/50), especially for manipulating and switching between windows and for displaying menus. Certain interface features are annoying. For example, new windows usually appear at random screen locations, and several standard Sunview objects are difficult to use (e.g., scroll bars are functionally overloaded). From the programmer's perspective, it is easy to create applications that follow standard Sunview utilities. However, altering the interface look or behavior is considered difficult. Greenberg, Peterson, and Witten (1986) discuss broader issues in the design of window management systems.

9.1.2 An overview of WORKBENCH

The rest of this section describes WORKBENCH. Because print on paper is a poor medium for explaining highly interactive systems, snapshots of the workstation screen are used to help convey the nature of the interface. The text is also annotated with notes indicating why design decisions were made and listing some of the problems encountered.

WORKBENCH loosely follows the metaphor of a handyman's real workbench. It has three visual components on permanent display, presented as the three horizontally tiled sub-windows illustrated and labeled in Figure 9.1. These are the *work surface*, the *tool area*, and the *tool cabinet*. When the WORKBENCH frame is closed, it shrinks to a pictogram of a physical workbench, shown by the icon at the top left of Figure 9.1.

The *work surface* is the tty sub-window on the bottom running *csh*, and it is the

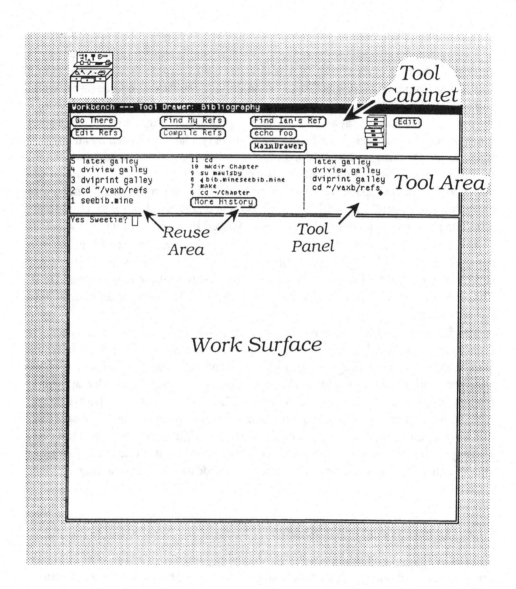

Figure 9.1. The normal appearance of the WORKBENCH window.

main working area on workbench. When it is selected as the focus of attention, all lines entered through typing are processed by *csh* in the usual way.

The middle sub-window is the *tool area*. It includes a *reuse facility* for storing, selecting, and editing lines entered to *csh*, and a *tool panel* for keeping several activities on hand independent of history. The tool area is analogous to the surfaces surrounding a real workbench where recently used and favored tools are kept on hand. It is a Sunview panel that includes three columns of text items and a button (Figure 9.1). The first two columns are the reuse facility, and up to eleven lines from a history list of *csh* input are displayed there. The third column makes up the tool panel where up to six favored activities can be stored. Selecting any text item with the middle mouse button inserts the text into the work surface, which results in its execution by *csh*. The left mouse button enables editing, copying, and pasting – a left-key press highlights the text and internally stores it in a copy buffer, whereas a shift-left pastes the stored string into a new text item.[3] Through copy and paste, the user can move text from the dynamic history list to the static tool panel.

> *Note 1.* The use of text items by WORKBENCH is non-standard, for Sunview does not consider them to be buttons. An alternative design could place a real button next to every text item and use that for selection instead. However, this adds complexity to the interface and also consumes more screen space.

> *Note 2.* Although button actions are invoked by clicking the left key on the mouse, text items use the middle key for an equivalent action. This is inconsistent. Switching the text item's left and middle key responses is not a solution, for it would make WORKBENCH's treatment of text items inconsistent with other applications. Neither design is satisfactory.

The *tool cabinet* is situated in the top sub-window of Figure 9.1. Through it, the user may open and display one of the many *tool drawers* available. Drawers contain both *tools* and *drawer handles*. Both are represented as labeled buttons distinguished by different text fonts. Selecting a tool inserts a UNIX command line into the worksurface sub-window, whereas choosing a drawer handle opens a new drawer in the cabinet, replacing the current one. The cabinet icon on the right allows the user to cycle through the drawers just visited (left mouse button), and to review and select from a menu of the drawers opened in the current login session or of all drawers available on the system (right mouse button). Finally, selecting the *edit* button on the panel's right pops up a frame containing an editable representation of the current drawer.

---

[3]This violates the Sunview copy/paste standard, which uses a facility called the selection service. Only time constraints prevented its proper implementation here.

Note 3. WORKBENCH by itself is not meant to handle all task switching properties addressed by a workspace. Rather, it should be available as a window within a ROOMS-style environment (Section 8.3). Whereas ROOMS provides ways of collecting and switching between windows and their associated applications, WORKBENCH provides ways of maintaining and organizing application- and task-specific details within a window. Due to time constraints, a ROOMS-style environment was not implemented around WORKBENCH.

9.1.3 Designing the tool area

Eleven previous submissions are always available for selection in the reuse portion of the tool area (Figure 9.1). The submissions presented are continuously updated to correspond to a history list maintained internally by WORKBENCH. The numbering corresponds to the order of items maintained on the history list (e.g., item 1 has just been entered). These items are presented in a fish-eye view, where the font size of the text decreases with its probability of selection. If the user wishes to view more than eleven items, he may choose the *More History* button, which raises a pop-up frame containing thirty-nine further predictions (Figure 9.2, right side).

Note 4. Given the findings of previous chapters, eleven items seems a reasonable number. They do not consume much screen space and there is little gained from adding more. Eleven choices may be too many.

Note 5. The fish-eye view is a tradeoff between legibility and screen area. Although the more probable items are easily read, the small size of items in the second column may preclude their use. Unfortunately, control of font size is not as rich as it could be – only three are available in Sunview.

Note 6. The reuse list is numbered and read from the bottom up. Although top-down presentation may seem intuitively more natural, the current ordering and addition of new items follows the scrolling direction of the text in the work surface.

The history list of *csh* input lines can be presented in several ways. By default, previous submissions are presented as a recency-ordered list with duplicates removed. Alternatively, the user may request duplicate items to be shown by toggling the cycle choice item on the *workbench property sheet* sub-frame – raised through a pop-up menu attached to the *More History* button – illustrated near the bottom of Figure 9.2. The user can also display command-sensitive sub-lists by raising a context-sensitive menu attached to all text items. Figure 9.2, for example, shows the sub-list for all the different ways the user has submitted the frequently

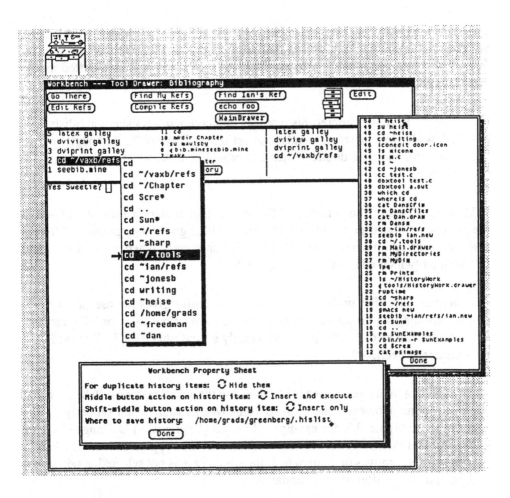

Figure 9.2. Ancillary controls of the tool area.

used *cd* command. The menu also displays the full view of the current selection, which is important for long strings that are not completely visible within the text item. The expansion alone is also available through a non-standard shifted mouse right-key press.

> *Note 7.* Recency-ordered history lists and command-sensitive sub-lists follow the design recommendations set out in Chapter 7. Although an option for showing duplicate items is provided, it seems unnecessary in practice.

Users may change the behavior of the middle button key on a text item through the above-mentioned pop-up property sheet. Although the key press will always insert the text into the work surface, the user can specify whether the line should be executed (which adds a terminating line feed).

> *Note 8.* Insertion without execution theoretically gives the user a way of avoiding an erroneous selection by allowing time to reconsider the choice. But error handling is not so easily solved; this issue is discussed further in Section 9.2.

Any text item in the reuse area is editable, and the edited version will be executed upon selection. However, the original form will be maintained properly on the history list. In Figure 9.2, for example, if item 5 (*latex galley*) is changed to *latex galley-test* and then selected, the new version will then appear as item 1, whereas the original form moves on to item 6. If the edited item is not selected, it will revert to the original text after the next update.

> *Note 9.* As previously mentioned, Suntool text items have poor editing capabilities. This is frustrating, for even simple text modifications are tedious and usually not worth the bother. The only real value of editing is that text is easily appended to an item (which supports the partial matching by prefix method, Section 6.1.2). Sunview will support proper editing in the near future.

WORKBENCH remembers its current state between sessions in several files. By default, history is saved in one location only. However, the user can also save (and optionally restore) the history in different files through the workbench property sheet (Figure 9.2). For example, using a relative file name will make the history list directory-sensitive on start-up. Through a pop-up menu attached to the *More History* button (not shown), one can save, clear, or load the history from or to a file at any time during the session.

Note 10. Chapter 7 indicates that directory-sensitive history lists provide some predictive benefit. Although saving history in different files lets users open workbenches primed to certain activities, this probably will not be used. Directory-sensitivity should be integrated properly as an option in the next version of WORKBENCH.

Finally, users can type or copy executable lines from the reuse area into any one of the editable six text items in the tool panel. The text remains in place until it is next edited by the user, that is, it acts as a tool cache. Copying is fast; several items can be transferred in a few seconds. Furthermore, items in the tool panel respond to mouse selections in exactly the same way as do text items in the reuse area.

Note 11. An alternate design of the tool panel considered placing history selections into empty slots, taking advantage of the fact that users continually recall the same activity when using history (Section 7.1.1). This feature was not included due to the danger of overloading the tool panel's functionality.

9.1.4 Designing the tool cabinet

The tool cabinet displays a drawer at a time. The drawer's name appears in the title bar of the WORKBENCH frame, and its contents are located in the top sub-window. Entries in a tool cabinet drawer comprise four types, where three are presented as text buttons and one as a pictogram. The first is a *tool* that invokes a Unix command, which is inserted and executed in the work surface upon button selection. The second is a *drawer handle*, whose selection will close the current drawer and open a new one. The other two are special-purpose edit and cabinet buttons.

A tool has three internal components: an executable string, a short label, and some help text that describes the tool's function. Only the executable string is mandatory. Tool buttons display the label (if there is one), or as much of the executable string as will fit. At any time, the user can raise a help menu that displays the help text (if any is available) and the executable command. Figure 9.3 illustrates the help menu for the tool button labeled *Edit Refs*. The help string *Edit my refer file* appears as the first menu item, followed by the executable string *gmacs new*. The user invokes *gmacs new* by either clicking on the button or selecting it from the help menu.

A drawer handle has only two components: a short label that is also the name of the drawer to be opened, and a help string. The label is displayed in a serifed font to distinguish it visually from the sans-serifed tool button. The help menu works the same way as the one described above, except that no action is displayed. The button labeled *MainDrawer* in Figures 9.2 and 9.3 is one example of a drawer

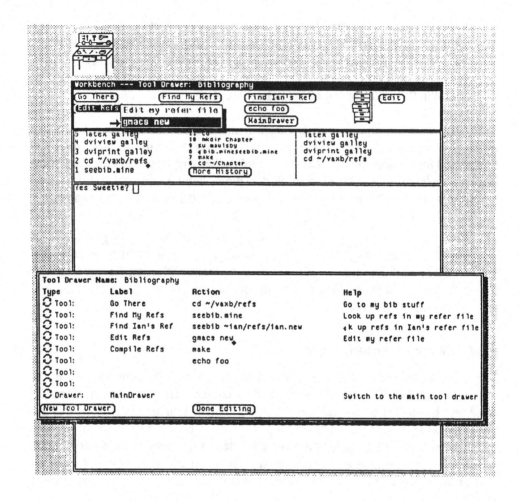

Figure 9.3. Ancillary controls of the cabinet.

handle. If it were selected, the entries of the current *Bibliography* drawer would be replaced by the ones from *MainDrawer*. The title bar is also updated to reflect the drawer's name.

The cabinet pictogram is a button that offers another navigation scheme for drawers. Raising its menu shows a trail of all drawers visited. As with the reuse area, open drawers are maintained as a recency-ordered history list without duplicates. The user can choose a menu item to return to any previous drawer. Alternatively, clicking on the cabinet button will cycle back through the history list one drawer at a time. The user may also view and select any drawer available on the system through a menu raised via the middle mouse key.

Central to WORKBENCH is the method of creating and altering the drawers and the items they contain. Without the ability to personalize it, the cabinet would be of limited novelty and would contain no fundamentally new ideas, thus being simply a way of allowing users to navigate through a predetermined network of utilities. But the inclusion of an end-user creation/maintenance system provides an interesting medium in which to explore explicit user personalization in a rather sophisticated interface. It is essential to success that modification be quick and easy, for if not, novice users will be denied access to a tool that should make work much easier for them, and expert users will not alter the support structure to reflect changing requirements.

The user defines drawers in the first place by filling out and editing a simple form, raised as a pop-up window by selecting the *edit* button on the tool cabinet (Figure 9.3). The top line of the form shows the name of the drawer, whereas each subsequent line represents the attributes of a single drawer button. The choice item sets the button type as either a tool or a drawer handle. The three other fields in the line are editable panel text items that specify the label, action (for tools only), and help associated with each button. Figure 9.3 shows a snapshot of WORKBENCH with the current *Bibliography* drawer opened for editing. The relation between the drawer's items as shown in the cabinet and in the form should be self-evident.

> *Note 12.* Users are invited to document their tools when created by attaching a meaningful symbol to an action, and by annotating it with help. This ameliorates one of the most severe drawbacks to explicit personalization schemes – that a user becomes confused and disoriented when faced with another's model (and perhaps even with his own). Although there is no check that the user-supplied label and help information is accurate, the fact that it can be provided should encourage sensible use. However, attaching help to buttons is non-standard in Sunview.

A user edits or expands an existing drawer by traversing the network in the normal way and then selecting the *edit* button, which always displays the current drawer. New drawers are created by selecting the button labeled *New Tool Drawer* at the bottom left of the form and filling in the vacant fields as desired. Drawers are linked to each other by changing the item type to a drawer handle and filling in the appropriate name in the label slot. The user quits the editing session through the *Done Editing* button, and an alert box gives him the option of saving or discarding any changes made.

> *Note 13.* The user has no support for globally examining, modifying, or removing links between drawers. This lack is quite serious. Section 9.2 will discuss this deficiency and raise other general concerns of user-created networks.

> *Note 14.* If a user wishes to create an explicit link to an existing drawer, the user must recall and type it in, a highly error-prone activity. A better method would attach a menu to the label field of the drawer handle that lists all the drawers available and inserts the name selected.

A novel and necessary feature of the drawer editor is that activities can be copied from the history list or tool panel to the current drawer item. This is the same method used to transfer text within the tool area. In fact, lines can be copied from one text item to any other throughout WORKBENCH.

> *Note 15.* The current system follows the simple strategy of copying straight text from one text item to another, a clearly limited approach. One should be able to select and group multiple fields and multiple lines for copying as a single entity. This would reduce tedium for the user who, for example, wishes to package all his tool panel items into a drawer.

The drawer editor described here is a user interface prototyping scheme for creating simple interfaces with control panels. With it, end-users can easily and interactively build a window interface for a command-based interactive program. For example, a UNIX software tool with a plethora of switches to generate different variants of its behavior can in a matter of minutes be given a smooth, window-based interface that is controlled by buttons, each having pertinent context-dependent help. Similarly, activities surrounding a task can be pulled off the tool area and packaged as a drawer.

9.1.5 *Underlying architecture of WORKBENCH*

WORKBENCH is an independent UNIX process that communicates with application programs. Upon invocation, it creates a unique UNIX socket (Sun, 1986a), and then spawns a single new *csh* process. While WORKBENCH is listening for any messages sent to it, *csh* searches for and establishes one-way communication through the socket. WORKBENCH then becomes a receiver that collects historical activities directly from *csh*.

As a sender, WORKBENCH does not communicate directly with *csh*, but merely inserts text into the workspace. The current application receives the text as if the user typed it in himself.

> *Note 16.* Multiple applications running concurrently can be supported by this architecture, as WORKBENCH can receive messages from *any* process that sends to it (although only *csh* is used in this version). By maintaining and switching between different history lists, the presentation of activities on the tool area could then be application sensitive. This theme is expanded upon later.

History is maintained in a data structure that allows WORKBENCH to present the list rapidly under three conditioning methods: sequential order showing duplicates, sequential order with duplicates shown in latest position only, and as a command hierarchy with command-sensitive sub-lists. Although not particularly elegant, the data structure serves its purpose quite well. Figure 9.4 illustrates how some of the lines shown in Figure 9.1 are maintained. As shown, the true history order is maintained as a linked list, where each node (called a line node) points to its corresponding command line, maintained separately in a binary tree (far left of the figure). Many line nodes may point to the same line, because only one copy is retained. Displaying the n most recently entered lines is simply a matter of getting the lines attached to the first n nodes at the head of the list.

The method for retrieving n lines with no duplicates shown is slightly more complex, for it avoids pattern matching as a method to determine if something has been seen before. It relies upon integer markers stored with every line in the binary tree and a single global counter, all initialized with values of zero when WORKBENCH is first invoked. Detecting duplicates is straightforward when each is set appropriately. When the view of the history list is to be updated, the global counter is first incremented to make sure that its value differs from all markers. Each line node is then visited in order. If the marker and counter differ, the item is presented and the marker set equal to the counter. If they have the same value, then the item has already been presented. The process terminates when the required number of items are found or when the history list is exhausted. There is no need to update nodes that have not been visited.

Command-sensitive sub-lists are maintained separately by using two additional binary trees (Figure 9.4, right side). One stores unique copies of all the commands (i.e., first words in lines) seen so far, whereas the other contains all arguments (remainder of lines). Every node in the binary tree of commands maintains a recency-ordered linked list of pointers to the appropriate arguments in the other tree. This becomes the command-sensitive sub-list. Because every line node

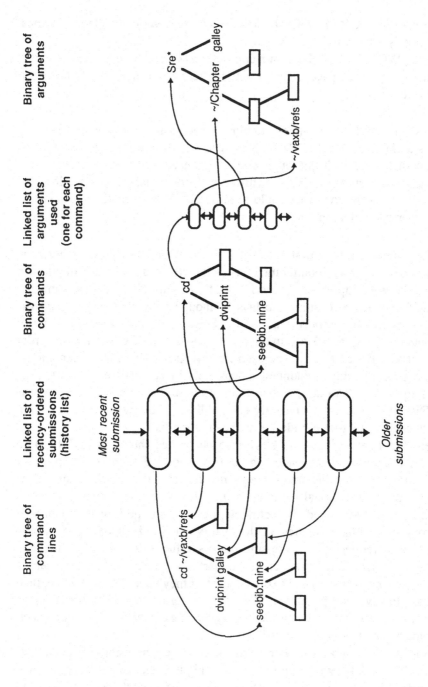

Figure 9.4. The data structure used to maintain the history list of activities.

also points to its corresponding command node, finding and retrieving the list of arguments is fast. Figure 9.4, for example, shows how the last three arguments used by the *cd* command are stored (also displayed in pop-up menu of Figure 9.2). Duplicates are processed in exactly the same way as the duplicate-removed history list mentioned previously. Again, no pattern matching is required to update the list.

> *Note 17.* Presenting and updating the history list is quite rapid, even when the auxiliary pop-up history panel is displayed. The user does not have to wait for the system to catch up with him. Similarly, the command-sensitive menu appears almost instantly. But given the speed of most window-based workstations and the relatively small values of n and of items maintained in history, the data structure used may seem overly complex and unnecessary. However, an early prototype built on a Lisp machine performed poorly when items were maintained as a simple record of lines entered and retrieved through pattern matching.

> *Note 18.* Another and perhaps more elegant data structure uses a single history list that maintains all pointers internally. For example, one chain of pointers would lead through the true sequential order; another would bypass all duplicates, and so on. No counters need be maintained, as all information is provided by the links themselves. A hash table or its equivalent would be available for rapid indexing into the structure. Although this structure is slightly more efficient than the one used, it is slightly harder to code in the "C" language used for this implementation.

9.2 Pragmatic concerns and research questions

In the design presented here, a workbench metaphor was adapted for a user support tool that keeps recently used input lines available for selection and provides people with the capability of organizing their collections of lines. Yet several significant problems exist. First, serious engineering concerns arise from WORKBENCH being just a front end to an application. Second, several aspects of the design raise open research questions that need answering. Both themes are pursued in this section.

The lack of input redundancy. WORKBENCH provides a way of executing an input line by a single press and release of a mouse key. Because this eliminates input redundancy, it is quite difficult for the user to catch erroneous selections.

Consider a person who has written a document after removing an old one, where the actions displayed in the reuse area are *ls*, *rm document*, and *edit document*. After editing, the person decides to list the files (*ls*), but a sloppy selection mistakenly chooses the command that removes the newly created document. Destroying a day's work would certainly undermine one's confidence in WORKBENCH, and could discourage its continued use. The same argument applies, of course, to menus and buttons.

The problem of no input redundancy is not peculiar to this design, but plagues any system that allows users to invoke an action in a single step. One sometimes sees attempts to add artificial redundancy. The tool area, for example, can be set to insert a line into the work surface without executing it. The user can then preview the line and accept it by hitting the return key. Similarly, every choice could be confirmed through an alert box. Yet none are good approaches, for the act of acceptance often becomes a conditioned response. A better approach would include undo operations, of which many styles are available (Thimbleby, 1990). Users could then aggressively explore and pursue their actions, for they would know that they can backtrack to previous acceptable states at any time.

By itself, WORKBENCH cannot hope to solve this problem, for it is just a front end to an application that may not have an undo capability.

Collecting and presenting input from different applications. Reuse facilities must somehow collect a user's input before it can be presented. One architecture considered uses a pseudo-tty input filter that collects *every* line before it is submitted to the application, and passes a copy to WORKBENCH. This method is general-purpose and requires no modification of the source code of an application. However, it has several disadvantages. First, input to some applications may not follow the pattern of recurrent systems (e.g., lines of free text). However, their entries would still be collected and presented for reuse. Second, items from all applications would be presented together, even though it is unlikely that the user could make use of lines submitted to one application in another (e.g., *csh* vs. *lisp* input). Third, applications have no opportunity to massage input before passing it on. Errors cannot be treated differently, lines cannot be expanded, inappropriate submissions cannot be discarded, and so on. Effective reuse requires some applications to massage their input, because primitive activities may not be demarcated or well represented as a simple line. In *emacs*, for example, an activity could be an extended command line, which is denoted by an <escape-X> prefix. A hierarchical menu traversal may be represented by the name of the leaf node reached rather than (say) the function keys pressed.

For these reasons, applications should be responsible for collecting, massaging, and passing on a user's input. Non-recurrent systems would not do this, and the reuse facility would be made application-sensitive by maintaining and switching between various history lists. Yet this is impossible in the current UNIX environment. Source code is rarely available, and the task of modifying even a few key applications is daunting.[4] Clearly, an integrated system incorporating history collection primitives would have to be designed from the bottom up. The SYM-BOLICS Lisp environment is currently the only general-purpose environment that embeds and supports a uniform reuse facility across all applications (Symbolics, 1985).

User-defined symbols. The cabinet encourages users to label and add help to all their tools and drawer handles. Although intuitively appealing, there is no empirical evidence that this is a good strategy. Do individuals remember the meaning behind their labels over time? Are help annotations useful? Can a person use a cabinet created by someone else? These are all open questions.

Forming and maintaining drawers in a cabinet. The cabinet has no inherent structure of its own. Users can only list all drawers, or chase their own explicit links between drawers. Because a drawer can link to any other drawer, the navigation space is a network and is potentially complex. Yet it is not known whether personalized networks are usable in practice. Experimental evidence suggests, for example, that users of the UNIX hierarchical directory recall only half the names in their directory areas accurately after being out of touch with it for a lengthy period of time (Akin, Baykan, and Radha Rao, 1987). Users were also seen to develop search strategies for misplaced files. However, because the cabinet relies on recognition rather than recall, it is not clear how well the UNIX results apply. Again, these are open questions.

The navigational problems of a cabinet are potentially as complex as the ones found in hypertext systems, and call for an equivalent support structure. At the very least, the network should be portrayed as a graphical map that allows users to visit and modify the contents of drawers and their links through direct manipulation. Methods should be incorporated to ensure consistency on modification. For example, changing a drawer's name should be reflected by all links.

Generalization. Tools in a drawer (and possibly lines presented by the reuse facility) could have greater value if their parameters could be generalized. Currently, WORKBENCH only inserts a line into the work surface, and no facility is available to prompt for or to generalize its arguments.[5]

Generalization can be implemented by having the user explicitly mark a variable. Perhaps a prompt would be specified, defaults indicated, a list of available

---

[4]Obtaining, understanding, altering, and debugging the sparsely commented and undocumented source code of *csh* spanned a four-month period.

[5]This is not strictly true, for *csh* provides a way for a command line to get its input from subsequent input lines. For example, *echo "Show what file?"; cat $<* will print the prompt *Show what file?* and use the user's response as the argument to the *cat* command.

choices provided and displayed as a menu, the input limited to a specific type, and so on. Information could be presented and retrieved through a pop-up property sheet attached to the tool. Similar methods have already been implemented to elaborate programming constructs after creating a macro by example (Halbert, 1984). Perhaps the system itself could infer the generalization.

But are users, especially non-programmers, capable of specifying and maintaining these potentially complex behaviors of tools in a dynamic general–purpose environment? And is it worth their time and effort? No one knows.

10

Conclusion

If I send a man to buy a horse for me, I expect him to tell me that horse's points – not how many hairs he has in his tail.
—*Carl Sandburg's* Abraham Lincoln

This final chapter will be brief. First, the argument of the book is reviewed. Next, the original contributions are identified. Finally, new directions for research are sketched. The individual components of the book are not evaluated or criticized because this has been done at the end of each chapter.

10.1 Argument of the book

We began with the observation that orders given to interactive computer systems resemble tools used by people. Like tools, orders are employed to pursue activities that shape one's environment and the objects it contains. People have two general strategies for keeping track of the diverse tools they wield in their physical workshops. Recently used tools are kept available for reuse, and tools are organized into functional and task-oriented collections. Surprisingly, these strategies have not been transferred effectively to interactive systems.

This raises the possibility of an interactive support facility that allows people to use, reuse, and organize their on-line activities. The chief difficulty with this enterprise is the dearth of knowledge of how users behave when giving orders to general-purpose computer systems. As a consequence, existing user support facilities are based on ad hoc designs that do not adequately support a person's natural and intuitive way of working.

Admittedly, a few recent studies have analyzed people's behavior when selecting orders. However, closer examination shows that they concentrate exclusively on commands (the verbs of the human–computer dialog), and ignore options (the modifiers) and other arguments (the nouns or objects) of the command line. Consequently, a new study was undertaken to characterize people's behavior when selecting complete command lines.

Repetition of command lines deserved special attention, because of their potential for reuse. The problem is to identify likely candidates for reuse, and several ways of conditioning the distribution to enhance predictive power were evaluated. Several striking characteristics of how often people repeat their activities emerged from this study. They were abstracted from usage data gleaned from many users of different classes over a period of months. Reformulated as empirically based general principles, they constitute design guidelines for a facility that predicts old submissions for reuse. A case study of actual usage of a widely available history system provided a salutary reminder of the need for careful attention to design details.

So much for history and reuse. The next question was that of organizing activities by task and by function. An on-line facility called a "workspace" was described that allows people to gather together their tools for related activities. The problem is to identify the properties a workspace should have. Because our knowledge in this respect is limited, the properties were formulated as suggestions, and the list was augmented by creative ideas from existing designs that seem to capture some flavor of what a workspace should be.

Based on these suggestions, a system that loosely follows the metaphor of a handyman's workbench was designed and implemented. It includes a tool area made up of a reuse facility and a tool panel, where both recently used and explicitly cached submissions are kept available for immediate reuse. Through a tool cabinet, a person can organize his tools in drawers, and link drawers into a network by drawer handles. Any submission available on the history list can be copied and pasted into the tool panel or any drawer. Despite its principled design, the system illustrates that serious pragmatic problems are encountered when user support tools are bolted on to existing computer systems.

10.2 Contributions

Absolute originality in the field of human–computer interaction is hard to come by. A very wide spectrum of ideas has been mooted in one form or another; anyway, human–computer dialogs are analogous to human–human and human–machine ones that have been developing for eons and studied for centuries. For example, the idea of a reuse facility is clearly not new. Neither is the idea of a workbench. MENUNIX, ROOMS, and the SMALLTALK browser, surveyed in Chapter 8, can all be considered workbenches of one form or another. To find ideas absolutely original to this research, one must move to a finer grain of analysis.

There are two important fine-grained contributions in this book. One is the idea of conditioning history by command context to give better predictions. When combined with removing duplicates from the recency-ordered list, a full three-quarters or more of all recurring submissions can be chosen from a short history list (compared to two-thirds for a recency-only list). The quality of submissions presented is also higher, as measured by the length of text predicted. Because the order of submission entry is maintained, users can predict the system's offerings and its location on the list, and not waste time searching for items that are not there. The second contribution is the idea of using the history list as a primary source of tried-and-tested candidates for storage within the workbench organization. When combined with direct manipulation editing of workbenches (first mooted by

Greenberg and Witten, 1985b), people can rapidly create, annotate, and modify their personal workspaces so that they respond to their situated needs.

Aside from these two completely original contributions, there are a number of others which, though certainly important, have the character of more routine advances in human–computer interaction.

1. In surveying studies of UNIX usage:
   - faults and limitations of all data collection methods have been identified;
   - population statistics do not transfer well to individuals;
   - command lines are just as important as commands, if not more so.
2. In a new study of UNIX usage:
   - growth of a user's command vocabulary is slow and irregular;
   - growth of a user's command line vocabulary is rapid, linear, and regular;
   - recurrence rates for different groups, though different, are quite high;
   - the probability distribution of recurrences over a history list is strongly skewed toward recency of entry;
   - methods for conditioning the distribution can be ranked by predictive quality;
   - a case study of UNIX *csh* history indicates how poorly it performs.
3. In generalizing and validating the study:
   - a set of principled guidelines for reuse are offered;
   - testing a different system enforced the belief that these principles can be generalized.
4. In analysis of history systems:
   - reuse facilities are categorized and surveyed within a new taxonomy;
   - recurrent systems are defined, and UNIX *csh* is described in that context.
5. In the concept of workspaces:
   - people organize their on-line activities;
   - several design suggestions for a workspace are elaborated;
   - a principled design can be implemented on top of existing systems;
   - bolt-on user support facilities are not the complete solution.

10.3 Looking to the future

The scope for future research into reuse facilities and workspaces is large. The first step, of course, is simply to get these ideas integrated into future computing systems. In the next decade, I see a blending of the expert-oriented general-purpose environments of the seventies and the special-purpose appliance interfaces of the eighties, perhaps through a metaphor similar to the workbench. First-time and casual users will have a default workbench structure to begin with (created by the designer through discussion with users and analysis of their generic needs). It is a simple learning progression to go from modifying individual workbenches, to adding new ones, and finally modifying or creating new support infrastructures.

Of course, tool reuse and organization must be applied to the now-common graphical interfaces. We believe that many aspects of modern interfaces are little more than syntactic sugar extensions (but oh so sweet!) to command-based systems. After all, we see many applications that have literally hundreds of commands that are accessed via menu and button selection instead of typing. (For example, the MICROSOFT Word 4.0 word processor for the Apple Macintosh lists almost three hundred commands in its repertory.) Although recognition and entry of menu items is easier than remembering and typing commands, the user's task is still essentially the same. Menu selections appropriate to the task must be formulated, and the group of selections required remembered. An excellent recent foray into this area was made by Maclean, Carter, Lovstran, and Moran (1990), whose research parallels some of the work presented in this book. Their system provided users of the graphically oriented Xerox INTERLISP–D environment with tailorable buttons. In a manner similar to WORKBENCH, users could grab items off a history list, place it into a button, and then move the button anywhere on the screen.

The exciting possibility of workbenches modifying themselves (possibly through consultation with the user) would go even further to ensure their effectiveness. I foresee an intelligent interface monitor that keeps track of user activities and offers potentially useful workbench configurations on request. When combined with a knowledge base, the monitor may infer tasks and the collection of tools required from just a few user actions, possibly through stereotyping with existing models (Rich, 1983). One consequence is the rapid development of workbenches suitable for transient user actions. The next step, of course, is to use this infrastructure as a platform for coaching and advisory systems that detect bad task models and suggest alternatives.

There is still great scope for new research in user behavior. Although this book has made a start, little is known about how people use, reuse, and organize their on-line activities. Present reuse facilities leave considerable room for improvement, both in their user interfaces and in the predictive methods they incorporate. Other researchers are now extending the reuse strategies described here. As this book goes to press, Alison Lee from the University of Toronto is completing her doctoral dissertation on history tools for user support (Lee, 1992). In particular, she is examining the possibility that command line recurrences are local to a working set (akin to the behavior of memory references by computer programs; Denning, 1970), which may lead to an even better conditioning method than the ones proposed in Chapter 6. She is also investigating the tradeoff between the mental and physical effort associated with using history tools. At the University of Calgary, several researchers are investigating a variety of novel predictive methods, not only for reuse, but for programming by example systems (Greenberg, Darragh, Maulsby, and Witten, 1993). Still, our current knowledge of task formation and use is inadequate, and inferring a person's tasks from a trace is surprisingly difficult. It is not known how one person's collection of tools can best be shared with others.

The idea of a workspace metaphor is immature. Existing workspace implementations are not widely available, and not one has been scientifically evaluated. The viability of richly connected networks for organizing, linking, and browsing through materials is still an open question, which is now being addressed by studies of hypertext systems. Finally, surprisingly little is known about personalizable environments. This gap must be filled if people are to create their own symbols, annotations, and networks.

Tool use started when animals searched and used the debris of their natural environment to shape their physical world. It continues as people search and use the tools of their computers to shape and manage their own intellectual worlds.

A

A sample trace

A portion of a trace belonging to a randomly selected expert programmer follows in the next few pages. The nine login sessions shown cover slightly over one month of the user's UNIX interactions, and include 155 command lines in total.

As mentioned in Chapter 2, all trace records have been made publicly available through a research report and an accompanying magnetic tape (Greenberg, 1988b). This report may be obtained from the Department of Computer Science, University of Calgary, or the author.

Because the raw data collected is not easily read, it was syntactically transformed to the listing presented here. The number and starting time of each login session are marked in italics. The first column shows the lines processed by *csh* after history expansions were made. The current working directory is given in the middle column. Blank entries indicate that the directory has not changed since the previous command line, and the "~" is *csh* shorthand for the user's home directory. The final column lists any extra annotations recorded. These include alias expansions of the line by *csh*, error messages given to the user, and whether history was used to enter the line. Long alias expansions are shown truncated and suffixed with "...".

Command line	Directory	Annotations
Session 1: Mon Feb 23 16:09		
mail	~	Alias: /usr/ucb/mail
Session 2: Thu Feb 26 11:05		
man mklib	~	
man -k mklib		
Session 3: Thu Feb 26 22:06		
cd 500	~	Alias: ^cd 500 ; set prompt = "[$cwd:t] #!...
ls	~/500	
vhide		Alias: echo — .hide directory — ; ls ...
c		Alias: /usr/ucb/clear
ls		
e assign9		Alias: emacs assign9
spitbol assign9		
e		Alias: emacs
spitbol assign9		History used
e		Alias: emacs
vhide		Alias: echo — .hide directory — ; ls ...
lpr .hide/graph.spit		
cd .hide		Alias: ^cd .hide ; set prompt = "[$cwd:t] ...
lpr graph.spit	~/.hide	
lpr symbol		
cd 500		Alias: ^cd 500 ; set prompt = "[$cwd:t] #!...
ls	~/500	
e assign9		Alias: emacs assign9
e		Alias: emacs
spitbol assign9		
ls		
e		Alias: emacs
spitbol assign9		History used
e		Alias: emacs
spitbol assign9		History used
e		Alias: emacs
ftp vaxc		
ls		
more assign8.spit		
e assign9		Alias: emacs assign9
spitbol assign9		History used
e		Alias: emacs
echo poop > file		
spitbol assign9		History used
e		Alias: emacs
spitbol assign9		History used
e		Alias: emacs
spitbol assign9		History used

Command line	Directory	Annotations
Session 3 continued . . .		
e	~/500	Alias: emacs
ls		
e		Alias: emacs
spitbol assign9		History used
e		Alias: emacs
spitbol assign9		History used
e		Alias: emacs
spitbol assign9		History used
e		Alias: emacs
spitbol assign9		History used
ls		
rm assign8.spit *.bak *.ckp file		Alias: mv assign8.spit *.bak *.ckp file /...
ls		
e file1		Alias: emacs file1
cp file1 file2		
e file2		Alias: emacs file2
spitbol assign9		History used
e assign9		Alias: emacs assign9
spitbol assign9		History used
e		Alias: emacs
spitbol assign9		History used
e		Alias: emacs
more file3		
assign9		Error: system – permission denied
spitbol assign9		History used
e		Alias: emacs
ls		
more file3		
rm file3		Alias: mv file3 /.kill/
more file1		
spitbol assign9		History used
more file1		
e		Alias: emacs
spitbol assign9		History used
e		Alias: emacs
spitbol assign9		History used
e		Alias: emacs
spitbol assign9		History used
more file3		
more file1		
more file2		
e		Alias: emacs
spitbol assign9		History used
e merge.error		Alias: emacs merge.error
e assign9		Alias: emacs assign9
spitbol assign9		History used

Command line	Directory	Annotations
Session 3 continued ...		
more merge.error	~/500	
e		Alias: emacs
cat assign9		
∧Acat assign9		History used
		Error: execution – command not found
∧Acat assign9		History used
		Error: execution – command not found
cat assign9		History used
ls		
rm *.ckp *.bak merge.error file3		Alias: mv *.ckp *.bak merge.error file3 /...
ls		
script		
lpr typescript		
lpr typescript		History used
limits		
Session 4: Fri Feb 27 13:57		
cd 500	~	Alias: ^cd 500 ; set prompt = "[$cwd:t] #!...
ls	~/500	
e assign9		Alias: emacs assign9
ls		
rm *.bak typescript		Alias: mv *.bak typescript /.kill/
ls		
rm merge.error		Alias: mv merge.error /.kill/
rm file3		Alias: mv file3 /.kill/
ls		
cd		Alias: ^cd ; set prompt = "[$cwd:t] #! –>...
script	~	
ls		
lpr typescript		
Session 5: Fri Feb 27 21:50		
cd 510	~	Alias: ^cd 510 ; set prompt = "[$cwd:t] #!...
ls	~/510	
e rohl_machine.p		Alias: emacs rohl_machine.p
Session 6: Tue Mar 24 10:03		
prmail	~	
who		
ls		
l		Alias: ls -asl ;
morembox		Error: execution – command not found
more mbox		

Command line	Directory	Annotations
Session 7: Fri Mar 27 15:37		
cd 510	~	Alias: ^cd 510 ; set prompt = "[$cwd:t] #!...
lpr rohl_machine.p	~/510	
lpr rohl_compiler.p		
spit		Error: execution – command not found
lpq		
s		Error: execution – command not found
Session 8: Mon Mar 30 12:49		
ls	~	
prmail		
prmail		
cd herr/testass4		Alias: ^cd herr/testass4 ; set prompt = "...
ls	~yyy/testass4	
more README		
lpr test*		
limits		
ls		
more test1.rohl		
more test2.rohl		History used
more test3.rohl		History used
more test0.rohl		History used
more test0.rohl		History used
		Error: history – modifier failed
ls		
more test*		
cd		Alias: ^cd ; set prompt = "[$cwd:t] #! –>...
ls	~	
more type*		
ls		
cd 510		Alias: ^cd 510 ; set prompt = "[$cwd:t] #!...
ls	~/510	
Session 9: Wed Apr 1 11:08		
prmail	~	
cd 510		Alias: ^cd 510 ; set prompt = "[$cwd:t] #!...
ls	~/510	
more sillysort.rohl		
limits		

B
Summary statistics for each subject

The following pages list a few basic statistics observed for the subjects involved in the study. Each subject is identified by the name of his group and a number. For example, "Novice–1" is the first subject of the Novice Programmer group. These names match the file names found in the publicly available trace data (Greenberg, 1988b).

The statistics include each user's number of login sessions, the command lines entered, the different commands used, the *csh* errors noted, the times history was used, and the different directories accessed. For example, Novice–1 entered 2,457 command lines over fifty-five login sessions. Of those lines, 213 produced *csh* errors. History was invoked thirty-seven times, eighteen different directories were visited, and sixty-seven different commands were used.

Table B.1. *Statistics on Novice Programmers subjects 1–35*

Novice subject number	Login sessions	Total command lines	Different commands	Errors noted by *csh*	Times history was used	Different directories used
novice-1	55	2,457	67	213	37	18
novice-2	118	1,267	22	58	0	11
novice-3	345	2,337	26	93	0	1
novice-4	61	1,919	32	123	0	4
novice-5	62	593	24	67	0	5
novice-6	74	871	23	44	0	1
novice-7	94	1,039	38	51	98	11
novice-8	92	1,822	13	19	0	3
novice-9	44	853	26	63	0	6
novice-10	64	1,464	42	40	0	3
novice-11	59	256	26	21	2	1
novice-12	438	2,436	19	210	0	2
novice-13	49	652	20	49	0	2
novice-14	156	3,194	67	208	0	27
novice-15	79	1,139	14	48	0	1
novice-16	16	256	12	25	0	1
novice-17	135	1,194	23	59	0	1
novice-18	46	1,088	15	38	0	1
novice-19	103	3,401	59	363	7	4
novice-20	54	418	18	19	1	2
novice-21	44	849	22	42	48	3
novice-22	122	1,893	43	51	0	3
novice-23	90	2,138	30	72	0	2
novice-24	86	849	26	53	0	3
novice-25	169	2,066	13	217	0	1
novice-26	87	1,120	19	60	0	1
novice-27	71	1,195	25	63	1	9
novice-28	123	2,221	31	120	0	1
novice-29	94	1,230	14	44	0	3
novice-30	78	946	20	28	0	3
novice-31	64	2,073	27	102	0	7
novice-32	51	385	20	37	0	3
novice-33	199	3,127	31	106	0	6
novice-34	123	1,276	25	46	4	1
novice-35	90	1,444	22	54	0	6

Table B.2. *Statistics on Novice Programmers subjects 36–55*

Novice subject number	Login sessions	Total command lines	Different commands	Errors noted by *csh*	Times history was used	Different directories used
novice-36	141	3,213	55	137	0	5
novice-37	88	1,949	36	57	0	32
novice-38	109	839	12	17	0	2
novice-39	74	1,107	34	51	0	3
novice-40	58	967	17	24	0	5
novice-41	86	2,317	15	51	0	1
novice-42	92	1,068	31	33	0	3
novice-43	33	608	18	26	0	1
novice-44	59	1,277	14	40	0	2
novice-45	54	651	17	16	0	1
novice-46	276	4,163	120	372	112	58
novice-47	56	1,316	19	78	0	3
novice-48	23	269	12	9	0	1
novice-49	23	723	20	31	0	1
novice-50	48	985	33	92	0	3
novice-51	42	480	20	20	0	2
novice-52	69	650	22	38	0	3
novice-53	98	1,028	34	41	0	1
novice-54	38	683	19	56	0	10
novice-55	62	1,662	25	40	6	2

Table B.3. *Statistics on the Experienced Programmers subjects 1–36*

Experienced subject number	Login sessions	Total command lines	Different commands	Errors noted by *csh*	Times history was used	Different directories used
experienced-1	137	3,714	74	298	174	58
experienced-2	25	219	28	11	6	8
experienced-3	28	915	51	42	88	16
experienced-4	151	3,776	59	123	2	29
experienced-5	283	4,015	78	222	35	44
experienced-6	53	757	56	32	0	17
experienced-7	189	5,857	139	612	67	100
experienced-8	134	2,930	74	265	67	54
experienced-9	99	2,351	99	136	86	25
experienced-10	25	446	45	26	1	18
experienced-11	98	1,456	43	86	21	48
experienced-12	66	1,763	70	92	28	17
experienced-13	49	1,109	60	160	25	30
experienced-14	103	1,810	60	153	23	27
experienced-15	14	225	21	12	0	32
experienced-16	41	795	33	22	24	22
experienced-17	85	2,343	67	144	0	32
experienced-18	25	575	27	21	5	9
experienced-19	122	1,807	84	88	163	20
experienced-20	180	4,556	79	370	435	44
experienced-21	100	2,394	76	83	157	54
experienced-22	149	2,814	67	122	325	18
experienced-23	95	2,306	70	119	189	18
experienced-24	114	3,331	132	228	222	62
experienced-25	71	1,465	63	89	11	19
experienced-26	30	679	33	66	0	22
experienced-27	219	1,693	70	54	77	43
experienced-28	440	3,893	93	60	78	24
experienced-29	71	2,214	59	133	59	67
experienced-30	130	2,028	64	110	82	18
experienced-31	68	683	82	38	19	40
experienced-32	65	974	72	87	47	32
experienced-33	59	1,292	55	65	83	14
experienced-34	116	1,869	59	218	206	15
experienced-35	165	4,272	77	169	28	40
experienced-36	60	1,580	70	116	56	54

Table B.4. *Statistics on the Scientist subjects 1–35*

Scientist subject number	Login sessions	Total command lines	Different commands	Errors noted by *csh*	Times history was used	Different directories used
scientist-1	165	1,856	105	111	54	43
scientist-2	198	2,954	87	149	236	37
scientist-3	133	978	38	69	1	6
scientist-4	238	4,507	112	320	178	114
scientist-5	197	1,563	77	78	18	13
scientist-6	145	1,103	61	49	33	46
scientist-7	13	366	49	28	0	25
scientist-8	61	842	39	51	0	5
scientist-9	256	4,067	89	65	224	42
scientist-10	129	2,024	63	120	77	96
scientist-11	38	205	24	13	0	1
scientist-12	105	2,499	117	52	53	63
scientist-13	108	3,593	45	118	357	25
scientist-14	202	3,433	109	183	23	83
scientist-15	161	1,429	94	81	200	30
scientist-16	74	326	31	29	0	5
scientist-17	95	569	33	38	0	1
scientist-18	144	2,831	71	112	106	74
scientist-19	189	5,584	65	240	6	62
scientist-20	225	2,697	112	189	74	52
scientist-21	81	1,762	82	134	50	102
scientist-22	132	750	45	39	0	12
scientist-23	324	3,360	91	135	52	48
scientist-24	72	1,494	41	55	0	5
scientist-25	415	3,508	112	122	7	113
scientist-26	123	983	65	70	0	24
scientist-27	111	3,817	97	85	102	79
scientist-28	111	765	64	26	20	17
scientist-29	134	2,683	60	243	20	61
scientist-30	180	2,129	77	123	186	56
scientist-31	65	250	20	20	9	3
scientist-32	78	601	36	20	0	9
scientist-33	24	325	16	12	0	3
scientist-34	204	2,639	61	88	15	50
scientist-35	80	1,049	46	29	23	22

Table B.5. *Statistics on the Scientist subjects 36–52*

Scientist subject number	Login sessions	Total command lines	Different commands	Errors noted by *csh*	Times history was used	Different directories used
scientist-36	275	12,056	181	566	488	202
scientist-37	121	4,187	61	83	121	64
scientist-38	131	3,775	92	168	48	113
scientist-39	119	1,753	76	77	173	40
scientist-40	348	4,605	66	98	0	42
scientist-41	204	2,037	49	36	0	5
scientist-42	298	6,068	133	644	6	158
scientist-43	108	3,106	86	101	0	37
scientist-44	72	1,543	62	84	12	16
scientist-45	40	862	76	59	17	17
scientist-46	294	2,551	92	110	80	89
scientist-47	75	1,229	67	81	9	61
scientist-48	76	819	27	43	0	2
scientist-49	105	1,448	108	97	138	46
scientist-50	138	1,496	75	225	219	18
scientist-51	74	910	43	67	0	51
scientist-52	263	7,705	121	299	231	93

Table B.6. *Statistics on the Non-programmers subjects 1–25*

Non-progs subject number	Login sessions	Total command lines	Different commands	Errors noted by *csh*	Times history was used	Different directories used
non-progs-1	95	1,622	61	59	0	7
non-progs-2	53	454	16	15	0	2
non-progs-3	85	1,265	38	15	9	7
non-progs-4	133	5,050	70	161	18	89
non-progs-5	77	244	8	11	0	1
non-progs-6	23	177	17	7	0	2
non-progs-7	80	1,231	53	54	3	9
non-progs-8	23	239	32	13	28	14
non-progs-9	73	357	34	23	4	3
non-progs-10	32	495	36	20	0	21
non-progs-11	281	1,848	27	61	0	17
non-progs-12	24	216	19	26	0	4
non-progs-13	30	487	10	5	0	1
non-progs-14	17	201	9	4	1	3
non-progs-15	78	571	15	28	0	2
non-progs-16	46	821	32	26	18	11
non-progs-17	61	848	19	65	0	1
non-progs-18	97	1,403	22	64	0	2
non-progs-19	77	175	15	7	0	2
non-progs-20	137	4,042	81	124	165	30
non-progs-21	25	132	5	7	0	1
non-progs-22	151	1,567	39	56	48	8
non-progs-23	89	1,294	47	48	0	5
non-progs-24	35	542	25	34	0	1
non-progs-25	76	327	9	18	3	1

References

Akin, O., Baykan, C., and Radha Rao, D. (1987). Structure of a directory space: A case study with a Unix operating system. *International Journal of Man Machine Studies, 26*, 361–382.

Apollo (1986). *DOMAIN system user's guide*. Chelmsford, Mass: Apollo Computer Inc.

Bannon, L., Cypher, A., Greenspan, S., and Monty, M. (1983). Evaluation and analysis of users' activity organization. In *Proceedings of the ACM SIGCHI '83 Human Factors in Computing Systems*, pp. 54–57., Boston.

Bannon, L. and O'Malley, C. (1984). Problems in evaluation of human–computer interfaces: A case study. In *Interact '84 – First IFIP Conference on Human-Computer Interaction, 2*, pp. 280–284., London, UK.

Barnes, D. and Bovey, J. (1986). Managing command submission in a multiple-window environment. *Software Engineering Journal, 1*(5), 177–183.

Beck, B. (1980). *Animal tool behavior: The use and manufacture of tools by animals*. New York: Garland STPM Press.

Bennett, J. (1975). Storage design for information retrieval: Scarrott's conjecture and Zipf's law. In Gelenbe and Potier (Eds.), *International Computing Symposium 1975*, pp. 233–237., Amsterdam. North-Holland.

Bobrow, D. (1986). *HistMenu*. Lisp User Library Packages Manual, Koto Release. Xerox Artificial Intelligence Systems.

Bobrow, D. and Stefik, M. (1983). *The Loops manual*. Palo Alto, California: Xerox Corporation.

Bramwell, B. (1983). An automatic manual. Master's thesis, Department of Computer Science, University of Calgary, Calgary, Alberta, Canada.

Burton, R. and Brown, J. (1982). An investigation of computer coaching for informal learning activities. In D. Sleeman and J. Brown (Eds.), *Intelligent Tutoring Systems* pp. 79–97. New York: Academic Press.

Card, S. and Henderson Jr, D. (1987). A multiple, virtual-workspace interface to support user task switching. In *Proceedings of the ACM SIGCHI+GI 1987 Human Factors in Computing Systems and Graphics Interface*, pp. 53–59., Toronto.

Card, S., Pavel, M., and Farrell, J. (1984). Window-based computer dialogs. In *Interact '84 – First IFIP Conference on Human-Computer Interaction, 1*, pp. 355–359., London, UK.

Chan, P. (1984). Learning considerations in user interface design: The room model. Technical Report CS-84-16, Department of Computer Science, University of Waterloo, Waterloo, Ontario.

Chin, D. (1986). User modeling in UC, the UNIX consultant. In *Proceedings of the ACM SIGCHI '86 Human Factors in Computing Systems*, pp. 24–28., Boston.

Cuff, R. (1980). On casual users. *International Journal of Man Machine Studies, 12*, 163–187.

Cypher, A. (1986). The structure of users activities. In D. Norman and S. Draper (Eds.), *User centered system design: New perspectives on human–computer interaction* chapter 12, pp. 243–263. Hillsdale, NJ: Lawrence Erlbaum Associates.

Darragh, J. (1988). Adaptive predictive text generation and the Reactive Keyboard. Master's thesis, Department of Computer Science, University of Calgary, Calgary, Alberta, Canada. Available as Research Report 88/343/05.

Darragh, J. and Witten, I. H. (1992). *The Reactive Keyboard*. Cambridge series on human–computer interaction. Cambridge Unversity Press.

Darragh, J., Witten, I. H., and James, M. (1990). The reactive keyboard: A predictive typing aid.

IEEE Computer, 23(11).

DEC (1985). *VAX/VMS DCL concepts manual.* Maynard, Mass: Digital Equipment Corporation.

Denning, P. (1970). Virtual memory. *Computing Surveys, 2*(3), 153–189.

Denning, P. (1971). Third generation computer systems. *Computing Surveys, 3*(4), 175–216.

Desmarais, M. C. and Pavel, M. (1987). User knowledge evaluation: An experiment with Unix. In Bullinger, H. and Shackel, B. (Eds.), *Human-computer interaction – Interact '87*, pp. 151–156. Elsevier Science Publishers B.B. (North Holland).

Draper, S. (1984). The nature of expertise in Unix. In *Interact '84 – First IFIP Conference on Human-Computer Interaction, 2*, pp. 182–186., London, UK.

Dumais, S. and Landauer, T. (1982). Psychological investigations of natural terminology for command and query languages. In Badre and Shneiderman (Eds.), *Directions in human/computer interaction* pp. 95–110. Norwood, NJ: Ablex Publishing Co.

Dzida, W., Hoffmann, C., and Valder, W. (1987). Mastering the complexity of dialogue systems by the aid of work contexts. In Bullinger, H. and Shackel, B. (Eds.), *Human-computer interaction – Interact '87*, pp. 29–33. Elsevier Science Publishers B.B. (North Holland).

Ellis, S. and Hitchcock, R. (1986). The emergence of Zipf's law: Spontaneous encoding optimization by users of a command language. *IEEE Transactions on Systems, Man, and Cybernetics, SMC–16*(3), 423–427.

Engel, F., Andriessen, J., and Schmitz, H. (1983). What, where and whence: Means for improving electronic data access. *International Journal of Man Machine Studies, 18*, 145–160.

Feiner, S., Nagy, S., and van Dam, A. (1982). An experimental system for creating and presenting interactive graphical documents. *ACM Transactions on Graphics, 1*(1), 59–77.

Fellers, J. and Fellers, G. (1976). Tool use in a social insect and its implications for competitive interactions. *Science, 192*, 70–72.

Finlay, J. (1988). User expertise in a functional programming environment. Technical report, Department of Computer Science, University of York, Heslington, York. In preparation.

Fitts, P. (1951). Engineering psychology and equipment design. In S. Stevens (Ed.), *Handbook of experimental psychology* chapter 35, pp. 1287–1340. New York: John Wiley & Sons Inc.

Glinert, E. and Tanimoto, S. (1984). Pict: An interactive graphical programming environment. *IEEE Computer, 17*(11), 7–25.

Godfrey, D. and Chang, E. (1981). *The Telidon book.* Toronto: Press Porcepic.

Goldberg, A. (1984). *Smalltalk-80: The interactive programming environment.* Reading, Mass: Addison–Wesley.

Good, M., Whiteside, D., and Jones, J. (1984). Building a user-derived interface. *Communications of the ACM, 27*(10), 1032–1043.

Goodman, D. (1987). *The Complete HyperCard Handbook.* The Macintosh Performance Library. New York: Bantam Books.

Gosling, J. (1981). *Unix Emacs Manual.* Carnegie-Mellon University.

Gowlett, J. (1984). *Ascent to civilization: The archaeology of early man.* New York: Alfred A. Knopf.

Greenberg, S. (1984). User modeling in interactive computer systems. Master's thesis, Department of Computer Science, University of Calgary, Calgary, Alberta, Canada. Available as Research report 85/193/6.

Greenberg, S. (1988a). *Tool use, reuse, and organization in command-driven interfaces.* PhD thesis, Department of Computer Science, University of Calgary, Calgary, Alberta, Canada. Available as Research report 88/336/48.

Greenberg, S. (1988b). Using Unix: Collected traces of 168 users. Research report 88/333/45 plus tar-format cartridge tape, Department of Computer Science, University of Calgary, Calgary, Alberta, Canada.

Greenberg, S., Darragh, J., Maulsby, D., and Witten, I. (1993). Predictive interfaces: What will they think of next? In *Extra-ordinary human–computer interaction.* Cambridge University Press. In press. Also available as Research Report 91/448/32, University of Calgary, Alberta, Canada.

Greenberg, S., Peterson, M., and Witten, I. (1986). Issues and experiences in the design of a window management system. In *Proceedings of the Canadian Information Processing Society Edmonton Conference*, pp. 33–50., Edmonton, Alberta.

Greenberg, S. and Witten, I. (1985a). Adaptive personalized interfaces – a question of viability. *Behaviour and Information Technology, 4*(1), 31–45.

Greenberg, S. and Witten, I. (1985b). Interactive end-user creation of workbench hierarchies within a window system. In *Proceedings of the Canadian Information Processing Society National Conference*, Montreal.

Greenberg, S. and Witten, I. (1988a). Directing the user interface: How people use command-based systems. In *Proceedings of the 3rd IFAC Conference on Man–Machine Systems*, Oulu, Finland.

Greenberg, S. and Witten, I. (1988b). How users repeat their actions on computers: Principles for design of history mechanisms. In *Proceedings of the ACM SIGCHI '88 Human Factors in Computing Systems*, pp. 171–178., Washington, D.C.

Greer, K., Ellis, M., Placeway, P., and Zachariassen, R. (1991). *TCSH: Cshell with filename completions and command line editing.* (Version 6 ed.). Cornell University.

Hailpern, B. (1986). Multiparadigm languages and environments: Guest editor's introduction. *IEEE Software, 3*(1), 6–9.

Halbert, D. (1981). An example of programming by example. Master's thesis, Department of Computer Science, Stanford, California.

Halbert, D. (1984). *Programming by example.* PhD thesis, Department of Computer Science, Stanford, California.

Hall, K. and Schaller, G. (1964). Tool-using behaviour of the California sea otter. *Journal of Mammalogy, 45*(2), 287–298.

Hansen, W. (1971). User engineering principles for interactive systems. In *Proceedings American Federation for Information Processing: Fall Joint Computer Conference, 39*, pp. 523–532., NJ.

Hanson, S., Kraut, R., and Farber, J. (1984). Interface design and multivariate analysis of UNIX command use. *ACM Transactions on Office Information Systems, 2*(1).

Hecking, M. (1987). How to use plan recognition to improve the abilities of the intelligent help system Sinix Consultant. In Bullinger, H. and Shackel, B. (Eds.), *Human-computer interaction – Interact '87*, pp. 657–662. Elsevier Science Publishers B.B. (North Holland).

Henderson Jr, D. and Card, S. (1986). Rooms: The use of multiple virtual workspaces to reduce space contention in a window-based graphical user interface. *ACM Transactions on Graphics, 5*(3), 211–243.

Hoffman, C. and Valder, W. (1986). Command language ergonomics. In K. Hopper and I. Newman (Eds.), *Foundation for Human–Computer Communication* pp. 218–234. North-Holland: Elsevier Science Publishers.

Jorgensen, A. (1987). The trouble with Unix: Initial learning and experts' strategies. In Bullinger, H. and Shackel, B. (Eds.), *Human-computer interaction – Interact '87*, pp. 847–854. Elsevier Science Publishers B.B. (North Holland).

Joy, W. (1980). *An introduction to the C shell, volume 2c* (seventh ed.). Unix Programmer's Manual. Berkely, California: University of California.

Kernighan, B. and Mashey, J. (1981). The UNIX programming environment. *IEEE Computer, 14*(4), 25–34.

Knuth, D. (1973). *The art of computer programming: Searching and sorting.* Reading, Mass: Addison-Wesley.

Kraut, R., Hanson, S., and Farber, J. (1983). Command use and interface design. In *Proceedings of the ACM SIGCHI '83 Human Factors in Computing Systems*, pp. 120–124., Boston.

Kunin, J. (1980). *Analysis and specification of office procedures*. PhD thesis, Department of Electrical Engineering, MIT.

Kurlander, D. and Feiner, S. (1990). A visual language for browsing, undoing, and redoing graphical interface commands. In S. K. Chang (Ed.), *Visual languages and visual programming* pp. 257–275. New York: Plenum Press.

Leakey, R. and Lewin, R. (1978). *People of the lake*. New York: Anchor Press/Doubleday.

Lee, A. (1988). Use of history for user support. In F. Lochovsky (Ed.), *Office and Data Base Systems Research '88*. Toronto, Ontario: Technical Report CSRI–212, Computer Systems Research Institute, University of Toronto.

Lee, A. (1990). Taxonomy of uses of interaction history. In *Proceedings of Graphics Interface '90*, pp. 113–122., Halifax, Nova Scotia.

Lee, A. (1992). *History Tools for User Support*. PhD thesis, Department of Computer Science, University of Toronto, Ontario, Canada.

Lee, A. and Lochovsky, F. (1990). Study of command usage in three UNIX command interpreters. In L. Berliguet and D. Berthelette (Eds.), *Work with Display Units 89: Selected papers from the Second International Scientific Conference*. Amsterdam: North Holland.

Lewis, J. (1986). Analysing the actions of unix-users. DAI working paper 188, Department of Artificial Intelligence, University of Edinburgh.

Maclean, A., Carter, K., Lovstran, L., and Moran, T. (1990). User-tailorable systems: Pressing the issues with buttons. In *Proceedings of the ACM SIGCHI '89 Human Factors in Computing Systems*, pp. 175–182., Austin, Texas. ACM Press.

Maulsby, D. and Witten, I. (1989). Inducing programs in a direct-manipulation environment. In *Proceedings of the ACM SIGCHI Conference on Human Factors in Computing Systems*, pp. 57–63., Austin, Texas. ACM Press.

Maulsby, D., Witten, I., and Kittlitz, K. (1989). Metamouse: Specifying graphical procedures by example. *Computer Graphics*, 23(3), 127–136.

Maulsby, D., Witten, I., Kittlitz, K., and Franceschin, V. (1991). Inferring graphical procedures: The compleat metamouse. *Human Computer Interaction*, 7(1).

McIlroy, M., Pinson, E., and Tague, B. (1978). The UNIX time-sharing system: Forward. *Bell Systems Technical Journal*, 57(6), 1899–1904.

Miyake, N. (1982). Constructive interaction. Technical Report 113, Center For Human Information Processing, University of California, San Diego.

Myers, B. A. (1986). Visual programming, programming by example, and program visualization: A taxonomy. In *Proceeding of the ACM SIGCHI '86 Human Factors in Computing Systems*, pp. 59–66., Boston.

Nakatani, L. and Rohrlich, J. (1983). Soft machines: A philosophy of user–computer interface design. In *Proceedings of the ACM SIGCHI '83 Human Factors in Computing Systems*, pp. 19–23., Boston.

Nielsen, J., Mack, R., Bergendorff, K., and Grischkowsky, N. (1986). Integrated software usage in the professional work environment: Evidence from questionnaires and interviews. In *Proceedings of the ACM SIGCHI '86 Human Factors in Computing Systems*, pp. 162–167., Boston.

Norman, D. (1981). The trouble about UNIX. *Datamation*, 27(12), 139–150.

Norman, D. (1984a). Four stages of user activities. In *Interact '84 – First IFIP Conference on Human-Computer Interaction, 1*, pp. 81–85., London, UK.

Norman, D. (1984b). Stages and levels in human–machine interaction. *International Journal of Man Machine Studies*, 21(4), 365–375.

O'Malley, C., Draper, S., and Riley, M. (1984). Constructive interaction: A method for studying user-computer-user interaction. In *Interact '84 – First IFIP Conference on Human-Computer Interaction, 2*, pp. 1–5., London, UK.

Peachey, J., Bunt, R., and Colbourn, C. (1982). Bradford-Zipf phenomena in computer systems.

In *Proceedings of the Canadian Information Processing Society National Conference*, pp. 155–161., Saskatoon, Saskatchewan.

Perlman, G. (1984). Natural artificial languages: Low-level processes. *International Journal of Man Machine Studies, 20*(4), 373–419.

Pike, R. and Kernighan, B. (1984). Program design in the UNIX environment. *AT&T Bell Laboratories Technical Journal, 63*(8/2), 1595–1605.

Quarterman, J., Silberschatz, A., and Peterson, J. (1985). 4.2BSD and 4.3BSD as examples of the UNIX system. *Computing Surveys, 17*(4), 379–418.

Quercia, V. and O'Reilly, T. (1990). *X Windows System User's Guide*, volume 3 of *X Window System Series*. O'Reilly and Associates.

Reiss, S. (1984). Graphical program development with PECAN program development systems. In *Proceedings of the ACM SIGSOFT/SIGPLAN software engineering symposium*, Pittsburgh, Pennsylvania.

Rich, E. (1983). Users are individuals: Individualizing user models. *International Journal of Man Machine Studies, 18*(3), 199–214.

Ritchie, D. and Thompson, K. (1974). The UNIX time-sharing system. *Communications of the ACM, 17*(7), 365–375.

Ross, P., Jones, J., and Millington, M. (1985). User modelling in command-driven systems. DAI Research Paper 264, Department of Artificial Intelligence, University of Edinburgh.

Shneiderman, B. and Mayer, R. (1979). Syntactic/semantic interactions in programmer behaviour: A model and experimental results. *International Journal of Computer and Information Sciences, 8*(3), 219–238.

Sleeman, D. and Brown, J. (1982). Introduction: Intelligent tutoring systems. In D. Sleeman and J. Brown (Eds.), *Intelligent tutoring systems* pp. 1–8. New York: Academic Press.

Smullen, I. (1978). The chimp that went fishing. *International Wildlife, 8*(3), 16–19.

Stallman, R. (1981). Emacs: The extensible, customizable self-documenting display editor. *ACM Sigplan Notices – Proceedings of the ACM SIGPLAN SIGOA Symposium on Text Manipulation, 16*(6), 147–155.

Stallman, R. (1987). *GNU Emacs manual* (Sixth Edition, Version 18 ed.). Cambridge, Mass: Free Software Foundation.

Stefik, M. and Bobrow, D. (1986). Object-oriented programming: Themes and variations. *The AI Magazine, 6*(4), 40–62.

Suchman, L. (1987). *Plans and situated actions: The problem of human–machine communication*. Cambridge Unversity Press.

Sun (1986a). *Inter-process communication primer*. Mountain View, California: Sun Microsystems, Inc.

Sun (1986b). *Windows and window based tools: Beginner's guide*. Mountain View, California: Sun Microsystems, Inc.

Sun (1988). *The Sunview system programmer's guide, version 3.2*. Mountain View, California: Sun Microsystems, Inc.

Sun (1990). *DeskSet environment reference guide, Revision A*. Mountain View, California: Sun Microsystems.

Sutcliffe, A. and Old, A. (1987). Do users know they have user models? Some experiences in the practice of user modelling. In Bullinger, H. and Shackel, B. (Eds.), *Human-computer interaction – Interact '87*, pp. 35–41. Elsevier Science Publishers B.B. (North Holland).

Symbolics (1985). *User's Guide to Symbolics Computers, Volume 1*. Symbolics, Inc.

Teitelman, W. and Masinter, L. (1981). The Interlisp programming environment. *IEEE Computer, 14*(4), 25–34.

Thimbleby, H. (1980). Dialogue determination. *International Journal of Man Machine Studies, 13*.

Thimbleby, H. (1990). *User interface design*. New York: ACM Press, Addison Wesley.

Toyn, I. and Runciman, C. (1988). Glide: An exploratory programming environment for a lazy functional programming language. Technical report, Department of Computer Science, University of York, Heslington, York. In preparation.

Unipress (1986). *UniPress Emacs screen editor: User's guide*. Edison, NJ: Unipress Software Inc.

van Lawick-Goodall, J. and van Lawick, H. (1968). Tool-using bird: The Egyptian vulture. *National Geographic Magazine, 133,* 631–641.

Vitter, J. (1984). US&R: A new framework for redoing. *IEEE Software, 1*(4), 39–52.

Waite, M. (1987). *UNIX papers for UNIX developers and power users*. Indianapolis, Indiana: Howard W. Sams & Company/Hayden Books.

Whiteside, J., Archer, N., Wixon, D., and Good, M. (1982). How do people really use text editors? In *Proceedings of the ACM SIGOA Conference on Office Information Systems*, pp. 29–40.

Williams, G. (1984). The Apple Macintosh computer. *Byte, 9*(2), 30–54.

Witten, I. (1982). An interactive computer terminal interface which predicts user entries. In *Proceedings of the IEE Conference on Man–machine Interaction*, pp. 1–5., Manchester, England.

Witten, I., Cleary, J., and Darragh, J. (1983). The reactive keyboard: A new technology for text entry. In *Proceedings of the Canadian Information Processing Conference*, pp. 151–156., Ottawa, Ontario.

Witten, I., Cleary, J., and Greenberg, S. (1984). On frequency-based menu-splitting algorithms. *International Journal of Man Machine Studies, 21*(2), 135–148.

Witten, I. and Greenberg, S. (1985). User interfaces for office systems. In P. Zorkoczy (Ed.), *Oxford Surveys in Information Technology, Volume 2* pp. 69–104. Oxford University Press.

Witten, I., MacDonald, B., and Greenberg, S. (1987). Specifying procedures to office systems. In *Automating Systems Development Conference*, Leicester.

Xerox (1985). *The Interlisp-D reference manual – Environment, Volume 2*. Xerox Artificial Intelligence Systems, Xerox Inc.

Zipf, G. (1949). *Human behaviour and the principle of least effort*. Ontario: Addison-Wesley.

Author index

Subject index

Printed in the United States
by Bookmasters

Printed in the United States
By Bookmasters